To

MATTHEW VO

From

BCDGD HTGTA

Date

01 JAN 2012

365 Bedtime DEVOTIONS for Little Boys

Freeman-Smith, LLC.
Nashville, TN 37202

The quoted ideas expressed in this book (but not scripture verses) are not, in all cases, exact quotations, as some have been edited for clarity and brevity. In all cases, the author has attempted to maintain the speaker's original intent. In some cases, quoted material for this book was obtained from secondary sources, primarily print media. While every effort was made to ensure the accuracy of these sources, the accuracy cannot be guaranteed. For additions, deletions, corrections or clarifications in future editions of this text, please write FAMILY CHRISTIAN STORES.

Cover Design by Kim Russell / Wahoo Designs
Page Layout by Bart Dawson

ISBN 978-1-60587-233-9

Printed in the United States of America

365 Bedtime DEVOTIONS for Little Boys

Introduction

A Message to Parents

What do you talk about when you tuck your little boy into bed at night? One of the things you probably talk about—and should talk about—is God's never-ending love for your son. And this book of devotionals can help.

Perhaps your boy's bookshelf is already filled with an interesting, spirit-lifting collection of children's books. If so, that means you're a thoughtful parent who understands the importance of reading to your boy. And, if you treasure the time you spend reading to him during those special moments right before he falls asleep at night, this text will become an important addition to his library.

This book contains 365 brief bedtime devotions, a year's worth of inspiration, wisdom, and assurance. If you have been touched by God's love and His grace, you already know the joy that He has brought into your own life. Now it's your turn to share God's message with the young boy whom He has entrusted to your care. Happy reading! And may God richly bless you and your family now and forever.

Bedtime Devotional 1

Jesus Gives Life

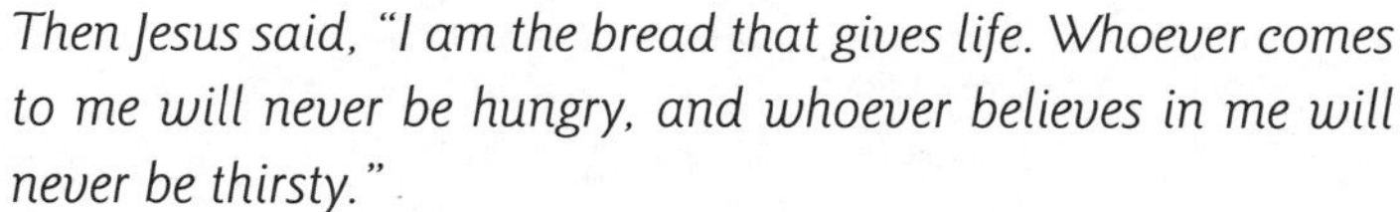

Then Jesus said, "I am the bread that gives life. Whoever comes to me will never be hungry, and whoever believes in me will never be thirsty."

John 6:35 NCV

Who's the best friend any boy has ever had? And who's the best friend the whole world has ever had? Jesus, of course! When you invite Him into your heart, Jesus will be your friend, too . . . your friend forever.

Jesus has offered to share the gifts of everlasting life and everlasting love with the world . . . and with you. If you make mistakes, He'll still be your friend. If you behave badly, He'll still love you. If you feel sorry or sad, He can help you feel better.

Jesus wants you to have a happy, healthy life. He wants you to be generous and kind. He wants you to follow His example. And the rest is up to you. You can do it! And with a friend like Jesus, you will.

Sleep On It!

Jesus is your true friend. He loves you, and He offers you eternal life with Him in heaven. Welcome Him into your heart. Now!

Bedtime Devotional 2

Ending Your Day with God

It is good to give thanks to the Lord, to sing praises to the Most High. It is good to proclaim your unfailing love in the morning, your faithfulness in the evening.

Psalm 92:1-2 NLT

How do you end your day? Are you one of those boys who falls to sleep without saying your prayers, or without thanking God for His blessings? Hopefully not! After all, God loves you very much, and He has given you many gifts. So the right thing to do is to thank Him every night.

Each new day is a gift from God, and every evening gives you another chance to thank Him for that gift. So bedtime is good to spend a few quiet moments thanking the Giver. Saying your prayers is a wonderful way to end your day.

Sleep On It!

Make an appointment with God every evening, and keep it. Reading your Bible and saying your prayers are important things to do. Very important. So please don't forget to talk with God every night.

Bedtime Devotional 3

Think Before You Speak

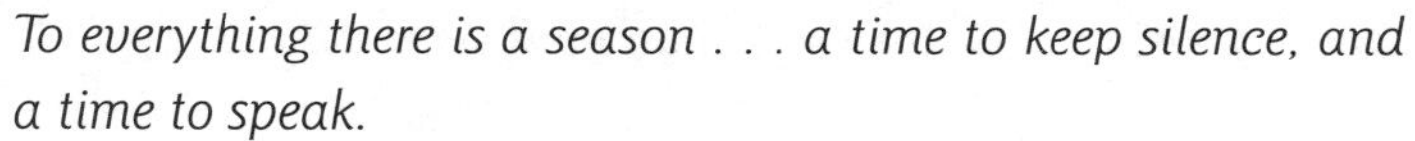
To everything there is a season . . . a time to keep silence, and a time to speak.

Ecclesiastes 3:1,7 KJV

Sometimes, it's easier to say the wrong thing than it is to say the right thing—especially if we're in a hurry to blurt out the first words that come into our heads. But, if we are patient and if we choose our words carefully, we can help other people feel better, and that's exactly what God wants us to do.

The Book of Proverbs tells us that the right words, spoken at the right time, can be wonderful gifts to our families and to our friends. That's why we should think about the things that we say before we say them, not after. When we do, our words make the world a better place, and that's exactly what God wants!

Sleep On It!

If you can't think of something nice to say . . . don't say anything. Sometimes, the best use of a mouth is to keep it closed.

Bedtime Devotional 4

Right and Wrong

Lead a tranquil and quiet life in all godliness and dignity.

I Timothy 2:2 Holman CSB

If you're old enough to know right from wrong, then you're old enough to do something about it. In other words, you should always try to do the right thing, and you should also do your very best not to do the wrong thing.

The more self-control you have, the easier it is to do the right thing. Why? Because, when you learn to think first and do things next, you avoid lots of silly mistakes. So here's great advice: first, slow down long enough to figure out the right thing to do—and then do it. You'll make yourself happy, and you'll make lots of other people happy, too.

Sleep On It!

Good behavior leads to a happy life. And bad behavior doesn't. Behave accordingly.

Bedtime Devotional 5

Time for God

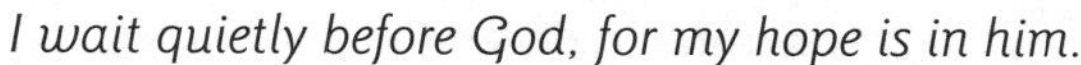

I wait quietly before God, for my hope is in him.

Psalm 62:5 NLT

When it comes to spending time with God, are you a "squeezer" or a "pleaser"? Do you squeeze God into your schedule with a prayer before mealtime, or do you please God by talking to Him far more often than that? If you're wise, you'll form the habit of spending time with God every day.

Even if you're the busiest boy on Planet Earth, you can still carve out a little time for God. And when you think about it, isn't that the very least you should do?

Sleep On It!

The world is constantly vying for your attention, and sometimes the noise can be deafening. Remember the words of Elisabeth Elliot; she said, "The world is full of noise. Let us learn the art of silence, stillness, and solitude."

Bedtime Devotional 6

Obeying God

But be doers of the word and not hearers only.

James 1:22 Holman CSB

How can you show God how much you love Him? By obeying His commandments, that's how! When you follow God's rules, you show Him that you have real respect for Him and for His Son.

Sometimes, you will be tempted to disobey God, but don't do it. And sometimes you'll be tempted to disobey your parents or your teachers . . . but don't that, either.

When your parent steps away or a teacher looks away, it's up to you to control yourself. And of this you can be sure: If you really want to control yourself, you can do it!

Sleep On It!

Associate with friends who, by their words and actions, encourage you to obey God.

Bedtime Devotional 7

Be Thankful

Our prayers for you are always spilling over into thanksgivings. We can't quit thanking God our Father and Jesus our Messiah for you!

Colossians 1:3 MSG

Are you a thankful boy? You should be! Whether you realize it or not, you have much to be thankful for. And who has given you all the blessings you enjoy? Your parents are responsible, of course. But all of our blessings really start with God.

All of us should make thanksgiving a habit. Since we have been given so much, the least we can do is say "Thank You" to the One who has given us more blessings than we can possibly ever count.

Sleep On It!

When is the best time to say "thanks" to God? Any Time. God loves you all the time, and that's exactly why you should praise Him all the time.

Bedtime Devotional 8

If You're Trying to Be Perfect

The Lord says, "Forget what happened before, and do not think about the past. Look at the new thing I am going to do. It is already happening. Don't you see it? I will make a road in the desert and rivers in the dry land."

Isaiah 43:18-19 NCV

If you're trying to be perfect, you're trying to do something that's impossible. No matter how much you try, you can't be a perfect person . . . and that's okay.

God doesn't expect you to live a mistake-free life—and neither should you. In the game of life, God expects you to try, but He doesn't always expect you to win. Sometimes, you'll make mistakes, but even then, you shouldn't give up!

So remember this: you don't have to be perfect to be a wonderful person. In fact, you don't even need to be "almost-perfect." You simply must try your best and leave the rest up to God.

Sleep On It!

Don't be too hard on yourself: you don't have to be perfect to be wonderful.

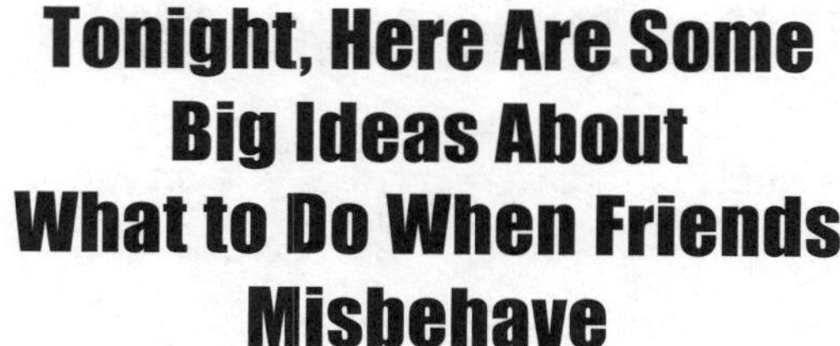

Tonight, Here Are Some Big Ideas About What to Do When Friends Misbehave

Here are two important ideas. Take a few minutes to talk to your mom or dad about what these quotations mean.

> God has a plan for your friendships because He knows your friends determine the quality and direction of your life.
>
> Charles Stanley

> A friend is one who makes me do my best.
>
> Oswald Chambers

Bedtime Devotional 10

Yes, Jesus Loves You

Just as the Father has loved Me, I also have loved you. Remain in My love.

John 15:9 Holman CSB

The Bible makes this promise: Jesus loves you. And how should that make you feel? Well, the fact that Jesus loves you should make you very happy indeed, so happy, in fact, that you try your best to do the things that Jesus wants you to do.

Jesus wants you to welcome Him into your heart, He wants you to love and obey God, and He wants you to be kind to people. These are all very good things to do . . . and the rest is up to you!

Sleep On It!

Jesus loves you so much that He gave His life so that you might live forever with Him in heaven. And how can you repay Christ's love? By accepting Him into your heart and by obeying His rules. When you do, He will love you and bless you today, tomorrow, and forever.

Tonight, Try to Memorize This Verse

For God so loved the world that He gave His only begotten Son, that whoever believes in Him should not perish but have everlasting life.

John 3:16 NKJV

This is an important Bible verse. Practice saying it several times. And then, talk to your mom or dad about exactly what the verse means . . .

A Tip for Parents

Tonight, talk to your child about . . .
God's infinite love.

Bedtime Devotional 12

Patiently Waiting

We can make our plans, but the LORD determines our steps.

Proverbs 16:9 NLT

God has a plan for you. But God's plan may not always happen in the way that you would like or at the time of your own choosing. Still, God always knows best.

Sometimes, even though you may want something very badly, you must still be patient and wait for the right time to get it, and the right time, of course, is determined by God. So trust Him always, obey Him always, and wait for Him to show you His plans. And that's exactly what He will do.

Sleep On It!

God isn't a talent scout looking for someone who is "good enough" or "strong enough." He is looking for someone with a heart set on Him, and He will do the rest.

Vance Havner

Bedtime Devotional 13

Respecting Others

Just as you want others to do for you, do the same for them.

Luke 6:31 Holman CSB

How should you treat other people? Jesus has the answer to that question. Jesus wants you to treat other people exactly like you want to be treated: with kindness, respect, and courtesy. When you do, you'll make your family and friends happy . . . and that's what God wants.

So if you're wondering how to treat someone else, follow the Golden Rule: treat the other people like you want them to treat you. When you do, you'll be obeying your Father in heaven and you'll be making other folks happy at the same time.

Sleep On It!

When dealing with other people, it is important to try to walk in their shoes.

Bedtime Devotional 14

Changing Habits

Do not be deceived: "Evil company corrupts good habits."

I Corinthians 15:33 NKJV

Most boys have a few habits they'd like to change, and maybe you do, too. If so, God can help. If you trust God, and if you keep asking Him to help you change bad habits, He will help you make yourself into a new person. So, if at first you don't succeed, keep praying. God is listening, and He's ready to help you be a better person if you ask Him . . . so ask Him!

Sleep On It!

The old saying is familiar and true: "First you make your habits; then your habits make you." So it's always a good time to ask this question: "What kind of person are my habits making me?"

Bedtime Devotional 15

Always Be Honest

The honest person will live safely, but the one who is dishonest will be caught.

Proverbs 10:9 ICB

Nobody can tell the truth for you. You're the one who decides what you are going to say. You're the one who decides whether your words will be truthful . . . or not.

The word "integrity" means doing the right and honest thing. If you're going to be a person of integrity, it's up to you. If you want to live a life that is pleasing to God and to others, make integrity a habit. When you do, everybody wins, especially you!

Sleep On It!

Unless you build your friendships on honesty, you're building on a slippery slope.

Bedtime Devotional 16

Getting to Know Him

If your life honors the name of Jesus, he will honor you.

2 Thessalonians 1:12 MSG

There's really no way around it: If you want to know God, you need to know His Son. And that's good, because getting to know Jesus can—and should—be a wonderful experience.

Jesus has an amazing love for you, so welcome Him into your heart today. When you do, you'll always be grateful that you did.

Sleep On It!

The crucial question for each of us is this: What do you think of Jesus, and do you yet have a personal acquaintance with Him?

Hannah Whitall Smith

Bedtime Devotional 17

Kindness Starts with You

Be kind to one another, tender-hearted, forgiving each other, just as God in Christ also has forgiven you.

Ephesians 4:32 NASB

If you're waiting for other people to be nice to you before you're nice to them, you've got it backwards. Kindness starts with you! You see, you can never control what other people will say or do, but you can control your own behavior.

The Bible tells us that we should never stop doing good deeds as long as we live. Kindness is God's way, and it should be our way, too.

Sleep On It!

In order to be a kind person, you must do kind things. Thinking about them isn't enough. So get busy! Your family and friends need all the kindness they can get!

Tonight, Here Are Some Big Ideas About Jesus

Here are two important ideas. Take a few minutes to talk to your mom or dad about what these quotations mean.

This is my song through endless ages:
Jesus led me all the way.
Fanny Crosby

There is not a single thing
that Jesus cannot change, control, and conquer
because He is the living Lord.
Franklin Graham

Bedtime Devotional 19

Perfect Love

For God so loved the world that he gave his only Son, so that everyone who believes in him will not perish but have eternal life.

John 3:16 NLT

The Bible makes this promise: God is love. It's a big promise, a very important description of what God is and how God works. God's love is perfect. When we open our hearts to His love, we are blessed and we are protected.

Today, offer sincere prayers of thanksgiving to your Heavenly Father. He loves you now and throughout all eternity. Open your heart to His presence and His love.

Sleep On It!

Love has its source in God, for love is the very essence of His being.

Kay Arthur

Bedtime Devotional 20

Setting an Example

Set an example of good works yourself, with integrity and dignity in your teaching.

Titus 2:7 Holman CSB

The Bible says that you are "the light that gives light to the world." The Bible also says that you should live in a way that lets other people understand what it means to be a good person. And of course, learning to share is an important part of being a good person.

What kind of "light" have you been giving off? Hopefully, you have been a good example for everybody to see. Why? Because the world needs all the light it can get, and that includes your light, too!

Sleep On It!

Think about the ways that your behavior impacts your family and friends.

Feeling Better

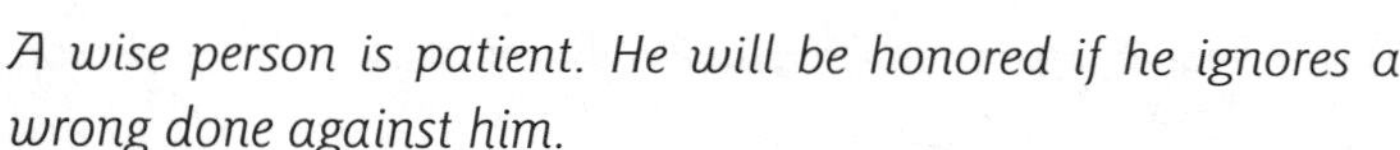

A wise person is patient. He will be honored if he ignores a wrong done against him.

Proverbs 19:11 ICB

Is forgiving someone else an easy thing for you to do or a hard thing? If you're like most people, forgiving others can be hard, Hard, HARD! But even if you're having a very hard time forgiving someone, you can do it if you talk things over with your parents, and if you talk things over with God.

Do you find forgiveness difficult? Talk about it and pray about it. You'll feel better when you do.

Sleep On It!

When God forgives, He forgets. He buries our sins in the sea and puts a sign on the shore saying, "No Fishing Allowed."

Corrie ten Boom

Bedtime Devotional 22

Solomon Says . . . Be Kind!

A kind person is doing himself a favor. But a cruel person brings trouble upon himself.

Proverbs 11:17 ICB

King Solomon wrote most of the Book of Proverbs; in it, he gave us wonderful advice for living wisely. Solomon warned that unkind behavior leads only to trouble, but kindness is its own reward.

The next time you're tempted to say an unkind word, remember Solomon. He was one of the wisest men who ever lived, and he knew that it's always better to be kind. And now, you know it, too.

Sleep On It!

Kindness should be part of our lives every day, not just on the days when we feel good. Don't try to be kind some of the time, and don't try to be kind to some of the people you know. Instead, try to be kind all of the time, and try to be kind to all the people you know. Remember, the Golden Rule starts with you!

Bedtime Devotional 23

Love to Share

And we have known and believed the love that God has for us. God is love, and he who abides in love abides in God, and God in him.

I John 4:16 NKJV

The Bible tells us that God is love and that if we wish to know Him, we must have love in our hearts. Sometimes, of course, when we're tired, angry, or frustrated, it is very hard for us to be loving. Thankfully, anger and frustration are feelings that come and go, but God's love lasts forever.

If you'd like to improve your day and your life, share God's love with your family and friends. Every time you love, and every time you give, God smiles.

Sleep On It!

God's love is our greatest security blanket: Kay Arthur's advises, "Snuggle in God's arms. When you are hurting, when you feel lonely or left out, let Him cradle you, comfort you, reassure you of His all-sufficient power and love." Enough said.

Bedtime Devotional 24

Choosing Wisely

I am offering you life or death, blessings or curses. Now, choose life! . . . To choose life is to love the Lord your God, obey him, and stay close to him.

Deuteronomy 30:19-20 NCV

Choices, choices, choices! You've got so many choices to make, and sometimes, making those choices isn't easy. At times you're torn between what you want to do and what you ought to do. When that happens, it's up to you to choose wisely . . . or else!

When you make wise choices, you are rewarded; when you make unwise choices, you must accept the consequences. It's as simple as that. So make sure that your choices are pleasing to God . . . or else!

Sleep On It!

Wise choices bring you happiness; unwise choices don't. So whenever you have a choice to make, choose wisely.

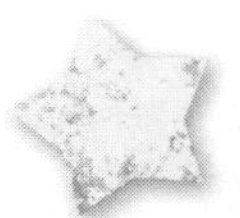

Bedtime Devotional 25

Your Attitude

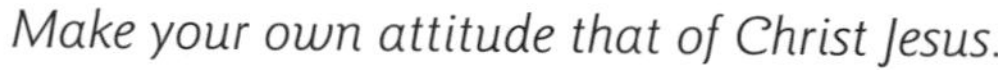

Make your own attitude that of Christ Jesus.

Philippians 2:5 Holman CSB

What's an attitude? The word "attitude" means "the way that you think." And don't forget this: your attitude is important.

Your attitude can make you happy or sad, grumpy or glad, joyful or mad. And, your attitude doesn't just control the way that you think; it also controls how you behave. If you have a good attitude, you'll behave well. And if you have a bad attitude, you're more likely to misbehave.

You have more control over your attitude than you think. So do your best to make your attitude a good attitude. One way you can do that is by learning about Jesus and about His attitude toward life. When you do, you'll learn that it's always better to think good thoughts, and it's always better to do good things. Always!

Sleep On It!

What will you pay attention to today? Try to pay careful attention to God's blessings, to God's love, and to God's rules. When you do, you'll be happier.

Celebrate!

Celebrate God all day, every day. I mean, revel in him!

Philippians 4:4 MSG

As you're getting ready for bed, will you take time to celebrate the good things that have happened to you today? Hopefully so! Are you expecting God to do wonderful things? Hopefully so! Are you happy about your family, your friends, and your church? Hopefully so! After all, God loves you, and that fact should make you very happy indeed. So treat this day as a big celebration . . . because that's exactly what it should be.

Sleep On It!

Every day is a cause for celebration: Psalm 118:24 has clear instructions for the coming day: "This is the day which the LORD has made; let us rejoice and be glad in it." Plan your day—and your life—accordingly.

Bedtime Devotional 27

Tonight, Try to Memorize This Verse

This is the day the LORD has made;
let us rejoice and be glad in it.

Psalm 118:24 NIV

This is an important Bible verse. Practice saying it several times. And then, talk to your mom or dad about exactly what the verse means . . .

A Tip for Parents

Tonight, talk to your child about . . .
the need to celebrate the gift of life.

Tonight, Here Are Some Big Ideas About Self-Control

Here are two important ideas. Take a few minutes to talk to your mom or dad about what these quotations mean.

> Your thoughts are the determining factor as to whose mold you are conformed to. Control your thoughts and you control the direction of your life.
>
> Charles Stanley

> God nowhere tells us to give up things for the sake of giving them up. He tells us to give them up for the sake of the only thing worth having—life with Himself.
>
> Oswald Chambers

Bedtime Devotional 29

The Best Excuse Is No Excuse

Each of us will be rewarded for his own hard work.

I Corinthians 3:8 TLB

What is an excuse? Well, when you make up an excuse, that means that you try to come up with a good reason that you didn't do something that you should have done.

Anybody can make up excuses, and you can too. But you shouldn't get into the habit of making too many excuses. Why? Because excuses don't work. And why don't they work? Because everybody has already heard so many excuses that almost everybody can recognize excuses when they hear them.

So the next time you're tempted to make up an excuse, don't. Instead of making an excuse, do what you think is right. After all, the very best excuse of all . . . is no excuse.

Sleep On It!

Making up a string of excuses is usually harder than doing the work.

Marie T. Freeman

Bedtime Devotional 30

God's House

For where two or three are gathered together in My name, I am there among them.

Matthew 18:20 Holman CSB

When your parents take you to church, are you pleased to go? Hopefully so. After all, church is a wonderful place to learn about God's rules.

The church belongs to God just as surely as you belong to God. That's why the church is a good place to learn about God and about His Son Jesus.

So when your mom and dad take you to church, remember this: church is a fine place to be . . . and you're lucky to be there.

Sleep On It!

Forget the excuses. If somebody starts making up reasons not to go to church, don't pay any attention . . . even if that person is you!

Moving On

Mockers can get a whole town agitated, but those who are wise will calm anger.

Proverbs 29:8 NLT

Are you the kind of boy who is kind to everybody? Hopefully so!

Tomorrow, and every day after that, make sure that you're a person who is known for the kind way that you treat everybody. That's how God wants you to behave.

And if someone says something to you that isn't very nice, don't pay too much attention. Just forgive that person as quickly as you can, and try to move on . . . as quickly as you can.

Sleep On It!

Be kind to everybody. Even when it's hard to be kind, it's worth it.

Bedtime Devotional 32

Keep the Peace

Love must be without hypocrisy. Detest evil; cling to what is good. Show family affection to one another with brotherly love. Outdo one another in showing honor.

Romans 12:9–10 Holman CSB

Sometimes, it's easiest to become angry with the people we love the most. After all, we know that they'll still love us no matter how angry we become. But while it's easy to become angry at home, it's usually wrong.

The next time you're tempted to become angry with a brother, or a sister, or a parent, remember that these are the people who love you more than anybody else! Then, calm down. Because peace is always beautiful, especially when it's peace at your house.

Sleep On It!

What if you're having real problems within your family? You've simply got to keep talking things over, even if it's hard. And, remember: what seems like a mountain today may turn out to be a molehill tomorrow.

Bedtime Devotional 33

Forgiveness Can Be Hard

Anyone who claims to live in God's light and hates a brother or sister is still in the dark.

I John 2:9 MSG

But God tells us that we must forgive other people, even when we'd rather not. So, if you're angry with anybody (or if you're upset by something you yourself have done) it's time to forgive. Right now!

But what if you have already tried to forgive somebody yet simply can't do it? Then you must keep trying. If you can't seem to forgive someone, you should keep asking God to help you until you do. And you can be sure of this: if you keep asking for God's help, He will give it.

Sleep On It!

Because God has forgiven you, you can forgive yourself.

Bedtime Devotional 34

The Very Best Time to Forgive Somebody Is Now

Working together with Him, we also appeal to you: "Don't receive God's grace in vain." For He says: In an acceptable time, I heard you, and in the day of salvation, I helped you. Look, now is the acceptable time; look, now is the day of salvation.

2 Corinthians 6:1-2 Holman CSB

When is the best time to forgive somebody? Well, as the old saying goes, there's no time like the present. So if you have somebody you need to forgive, why not forgive that person today?

Forgiving other people is one of the ways that we make ourselves feel better. So if you're still angry about something that somebody did, forgive that person right now. There is no better time.

Sleep On It!

When the Lord tells you it is time to do something (like forgive someone), the time to do it is now.

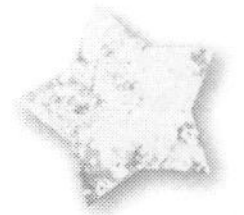

Bedtime Devotional 35

Let's Be Patient

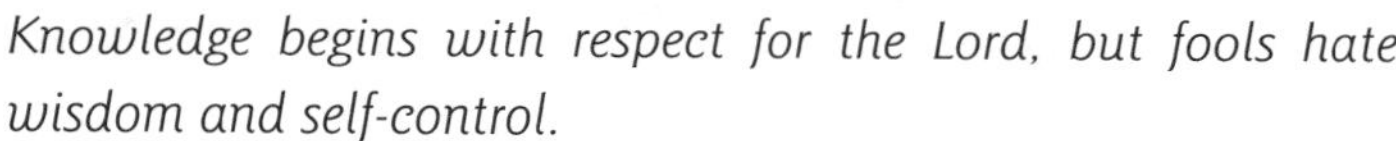
Knowledge begins with respect for the Lord, but fools hate wisdom and self-control.

Proverbs 1:7 NCV

The Bible tells us that we should be patient with everybody, not just with parents, teachers, and friends. In the eyes of God, all people are very important, so we should treat them that way.

Of course it's easy to be nice to the people we want to impress, but what about everybody else? Jesus gave us clear instructions: He said that when we do a good deed for someone less fortunate than we are, we have also done a good deed for our Savior. And as Christians, that's exactly what we are supposed to do!

Sleep On It!

Speak respectfully to everybody, starting with parents, grandparents, teachers, and adults . . . but don't stop there. Be respectful of everybody, including yourself!

Bedtime Devotional 36

Tonight, Try to Memorize This Verse

And remember,
I am with you always,
to the end of the age.

Matthew 28:20 Holman CSB

This is an important Bible verse. Practice saying it several times. And then, talk to your mom or dad about exactly what the verse means . . .

A Tip for Parents

Tonight, talk to your child about . . .
God's love.

Bedtime Devotional 37

About Barnabas

Barnabas was a good man, full of the Holy Spirit and full of faith.

Acts 11:23-24 ICB

Barnabas was a leader in the early Christian church who was known for his kindness and for his ability to encourage others. Because of Barnabas, many people were introduced to Christ.

We become like Barnabas when we speak kind words to our families and to our friends. And then, because we have been generous and kind, the people around us can see how Christians should behave. So when in doubt, be kind and generous to others, just like Barnabas.

Sleep On It!

Be an encourager! Barnabas was known as a man who encouraged others. In other words, he made other people feel better by saying kind things. You, like Barnabas, can encourage your family and friends . . . and you should.

Bedtime Devotional 38

Avoiding Mischief

Therefore as you have received Christ Jesus the Lord, walk in Him.

Colossians 2:6 Holman CSB

Face facts: not everybody you know is well behaved. Your first job is to recognize bad behavior when you see it . . . and your second job is to make sure that you don't join in!

The moment that you decide to avoid mischief whenever you see it is the moment that you'll make yourself happy, your parents happy, and God happy. And you'll stay out of trouble. And you'll be glad you did!

Sleep On It!

Christians are the citizens of heaven, and while we are on earth, we ought to behave like heaven's citizens.

Warren Wiersbe

A Wise King

If you need wisdom—if you want to know what God wants you to do—ask him, and he will gladly tell you. He will not resent your asking.

James 1:5 NLT

Solomon wasn't just a king. He was also a very wise man and a very good writer. He even wrote several books in the Bible! So when He finally put down His pen, what was this wise man's final advice? It's simple: Solomon said: "Honor God and obey His commandments."

The next time you have an important choice to make, ask yourself this: "Am I honoring God and obeying Him? And am I doing what God wants me to do?" If you can answer those questions with a great big "YES," then go ahead. But if you're uncertain if the choice you are about to make is the right one, slow down. Why? Because that's what Solomon says . . . and that's what God says, too!

Sleep On It!

God is voting for us all the time. The devil is voting against us all the time. The way we vote carries the election.

Corrie ten Boom

Tonight, Here Are Some Big Ideas About God's Love

Here are two important ideas. Take a few minutes to talk to your mom or dad about what these quotations mean.

> When once we are assured that God is good,
> then there can be nothing left to fear.
>
> Hannah Whitall Smith

> The love of God is revealed in that
> He laid down His life for His enemies.
>
> Oswald Chambers

Your Family Is a Gift

Love must be without hypocrisy. Detest evil; cling to what is good. Show family affection to one another with brotherly love. Outdo one another in showing honor.

Romans 12:9–10 Holman CSB

Your family is a wonderful, one-of-a-kind gift from God. And your family members love you very much—what a blessing it is to be loved!

Have you ever really stopped to think about how much you are loved? Your parents love you (of course) and so does everybody else in your family. But it doesn't stop there. You're also an important part of God's family . . . and He loves you more than you can imagine.

What should you do about all the love that comes your way? You should accept it; you should be thankful for it; and you should share it . . . starting now!

Sleep On It!

I like to think of my family as a big, beautiful patchwork quilt—each of us so different yet stitched together by love and life experiences.

Barbara Johnson

Bedtime Devotional 42

Everybody Makes Mistakes

Instead, God has chosen the world's foolish things to shame the wise, and God has chosen the world's weak things to shame the strong.

I Corinthians 1:27 Holman CSB

Do you make mistakes? Of course you do . . . everybody does. When you make a mistake, you must try your best to learn from it so that you won't make the very same mistake again. And, if you have hurt someone—or if you have disobeyed God—you must ask for forgiveness.

Remember: mistakes are a part of life, but the biggest mistake you can make is to keep making the same mistake over and over and over again.

Sleep On It!

If you make a mistake, the time to make things better is now, not later! The sooner you admit your mistake, the better.

Bedtime Devotional 43

Jesus Can Take Care of Our Problems

Do not love the world or the things that belong to the world. If anyone loves the world, love for the Father is not in him.

1 John 2:15 Holman CSB

An old hymn contains the words, "This world is not my home; I'm just passing through." Thank goodness! This crazy world can be a place of trouble and danger. Thankfully, your real home is heaven, a place where you can live forever with Jesus.

In John 16:33, Jesus tells us He has overcome the troubles of this world. We should trust Him, and we should obey His commandments. When we do, we are forever blessed by the Son of God and His Father in heaven.

Sleep On It!

If you dwell on the world's messages, you're setting yourself up for disaster. If you dwell on God's messages, you're setting yourself up for victory.

Bedtime Devotional 44

Becoming a More Patient Person

Be gentle to all, able to teach, patient.

2 Timothy 2:24 NKJV

The Book of Proverbs tells us that patience is a very good thing. But for most of us, patience can also be a very hard thing. After all, we have many things that we want, and we want them NOW! But the Bible tells us that we must learn to wait patiently for the things that God has in store for us.

Are you having trouble being patient? If so, remember that patience takes practice, and lots of it, so keep trying. And if you make a mistake, don't be too upset. After all, if you're going to be a really patient person, you shouldn't just be patient with others, you should also be patient with yourself.

Sleep On It!

An important part of growing up is learning to be patient with others and with yourself. And one more thing: learn from everybody's mistakes, especially your own.

Don't Copy Friends Who Misbehave

Stay away from a foolish man; you will gain no knowledge from his speech.

Proverbs 14:7 Holman CSB

If your friends misbehave, do you misbehave right along with them, or do you tell them to stop? Usually, it's much easier to go along with your friends, even if you know they're misbehaving. But it's always better to do the right thing, even if it's hard.

Sometimes, grownups must stand up for the things they believe in. When they do, it can be hard for them, too. But the Bible tells us over and over again that we should do the right thing, not the easy thing.

When your friends misbehave, it can spoil everything. So if your friends behave badly, don't copy them! And if your friends keep behaving badly, choose different friends.

Sleep On It!

Do you want to be wise? Choose wise friends.

Charles Swindoll

Bedtime Devotional 46

Learning to Control Yourself

But endurance must do its complete work, so that you may be mature and complete, lacking nothing.

James 1:4 Holman CSB

If you're having trouble learning how to control your actions or your emotions, you're not alone! Most people have problems with self-control from time to time, so don't be discouraged. Just remember that self-control requires practice and lots of it. So if you're a little discouraged, don't give up. Just keep working on improving your self-control until you get better at it. . . . and if you keep trying, you can be sure that sooner or later, you will get better at it.

Sleep On It!

If you learn to control yourself, you'll be glad. If you can't learn to control yourself, you'll be sad.

Bedtime Devotional 47

Tonight, Here Are Some Big Ideas About What Happens When You Pray

Here are two important ideas. Take a few minutes to talk to your mom or dad about what these quotations mean.

Prayer accomplishes more than anything else.

Bill Bright

Prayer succeeds when all else fails.

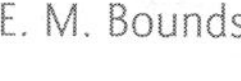

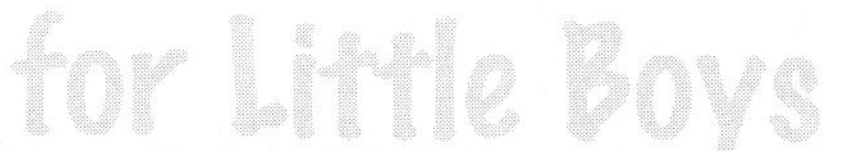

Bedtime Devotional 48

Patience and Peace

I leave you peace. My peace I give you. I do not give it to you as the world does. So don't let your hearts be troubled.

John 14:27 ICB

Patience and peace go together. And the words from John 14:27 remind us that Jesus offers us peace, not as the world gives, but as He alone gives. We, as believers, can accept His peace or ignore it. When we accept the peace of Jesus Christ into our hearts, our lives are changed forever, and we become more loving, patient Christians.

Christ's peace is offered freely; it has already been paid for; it is ours for the asking. So let us ask . . . and then share.

Sleep On It!

Patience is a virtue that carries a lot of wait.

Anonymous

Bedtime Devotional 49

Staying Out of Trouble

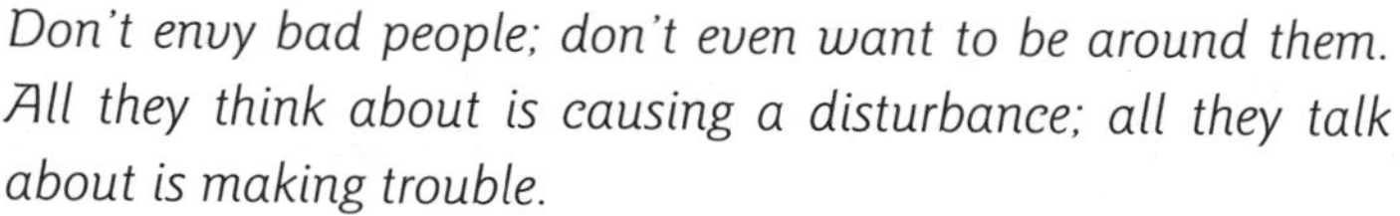
Don't envy bad people; don't even want to be around them. All they think about is causing a disturbance; all they talk about is making trouble.

Proverbs 24:1-2 MSG

One way that you can feel better about yourself is by staying out of trouble. And one way that you can stay out of trouble is by making friends with people who, like you, want to do what's right.

Are your friends the kind of kids who encourage you to behave yourself? If so, you've chosen your friends wisely. But if your friends try to get you in trouble, perhaps it's time to think long and hard about making some new friends.

Whether you know it or not, you're probably going to behave like your friends behave. So pick out friends who make you want to behave better, not worse. When you do, you'll feel better about yourself . . . a whole lot better.

Sleep On It!

For better or worse, you will eventually become more and more like the people you associate with. So why not associate with people who make you better, not worse?

Marie T. Freeman

Bedtime Devotional 50

Kind Thoughts

Whoever forgives someone's sin makes a friend, but gossiping about the sin breaks up friendships.

Proverbs 17:9 NCV

What does it mean to forgive? Forgiveness means that you decide to change your angry thoughts into kind thoughts. Forgiveness means that you decide not to stay mad at somebody who has done something wrong. Forgiveness happens when you decide that obeying God is more important than staying angry.

Sometimes forgiveness can be very hard, but it's the right thing to do. Why? Because forgiveness is God's way, and you should make it your way, too!

Sleep On It!

We cannot be right with God until we are right with one another.

Charles Swindoll

Working Together

Work at getting along with each other and with God. Otherwise you'll never get so much as a glimpse of God.

Hebrews 12:14 MSG

Helping other people can be fun! When you help others, you feel better about yourself—and you'll know that God approves of what you're doing.

When you learn how to cooperate with your family and friends, you'll soon discover that it's more fun when everybody works together.

So do everybody a favor: learn better ways to share and better ways to cooperate. It's the right thing to do.

Sleep On It!

Cooperation pays. When you cooperate with your friends and family, you'll feel good about yourself—and your family and friends will feel good about you, too.

Bedtime Devotional 52

Difficult Days

We take the good days from God—why not also the bad days?

Job 2:10 MSG

Face it: some days are better than others. But even on the days when you don't feel very good, God never leaves you for even a moment. So if you need assistance, you can always pray to God, knowing that He will listen and help.

If you're feeling unhappy, talk things over with God, and while you're at it, be sure and talk things over with your parents, too. And remember this: the sooner you start talking, the sooner things will get better.

Sleep On It!

When life is difficult, God wants us to have a faith that trusts and waits.

Kay Arthur

Bedtime Devotional 53

The Courage to Tell the Truth

And you shall know the truth, and the truth shall make you free.

John 8:32 NKJV

Sometimes, we're afraid of what might happen if we tell the truth. And sometimes, instead of doing the courageous thing, we do the unwise thing: we lie.

When we're fearful, we can and should find strength from friends, from family members and from God.

So if you're afraid to tell the truth, don't be! Keep looking until you find the courage to be honest. Then, you'll discover it's not the truth that you should be afraid of; it's those troublesome, pesky lies!

Sleep On It!

A person who really cares about his or her neighbor, a person who genuinely loves others, is a person who bears witness to the truth.

Anne Graham Lotz

Bedtime Devotional 54

It's Easy to Worry

The Lord himself will go before you. He will be with you; he will not leave you or forget you. Don't be afraid and don't worry.

Deuteronomy 31:8 NCV

It's easy to worry about things—big things and little things. But the Bible promises us that if we learn to trust God more and more each day, we won't worry so much.

Are you worried about something? If so, try doing these two things: first, ask God for His help. And second, talk things over with your parents. When you do these things, you worry so much. And that's good . . . VERY good!

Sleep On It!

Worried about something you said or did? If you made a mistake yesterday, the day to fix it is today. Then, you won't have to worry about it tomorrow.

Bedtime Devotional 55

Forgive . . . Quickly

Be even-tempered, content with second place, quick to forgive an offense. Forgive as quickly and completely as the Master forgave you. And regardless of what else you put on, wear love. It's your basic, all-purpose garment. Never be without it.

Colossians 3:13-14 MSG

When you make a mistake or hurt someone's feelings, what should you do? You should say you're sorry and ask for forgiveness. And you should do so sooner, not later.

The longer you wait to apologize, the harder it is on you. So if you've done something wrong, don't be afraid to ask for forgiveness, and don't be afraid to ask for it NOW!

Sleep On It!

Forgiving other people is one way of strengthening your relationship with God . . .

Bedtime Devotional 56

Friends Are a Good Thing

If you've gotten anything at all out of following Christ, if his love has made any difference in your life, if being in a community of the Spirit means anything to you, if you have a heart, if you care—then do me a favor: Agree with each other, love each other, be deep-spirited friends.

Philippians 2:1-2 MSG

The Bible tells us that friendship can be a wonderful thing. That's why it's good to know how to make and to keep good friends.

If you want to make lots of friends, practice the Golden Rule with everybody you know. Be kind. Share. Say nice things. Be helpful. When you do, you'll discover that the Golden Rule isn't just a nice way to behave; it's also a great way to make and to keep friends!

Sleep On It!

If you want to make more friends, how can you do it? Try this: First, become more interested in them . . . and pretty soon they'll become more interested in you!

Bedtime Devotional 57

Share Your Blessings

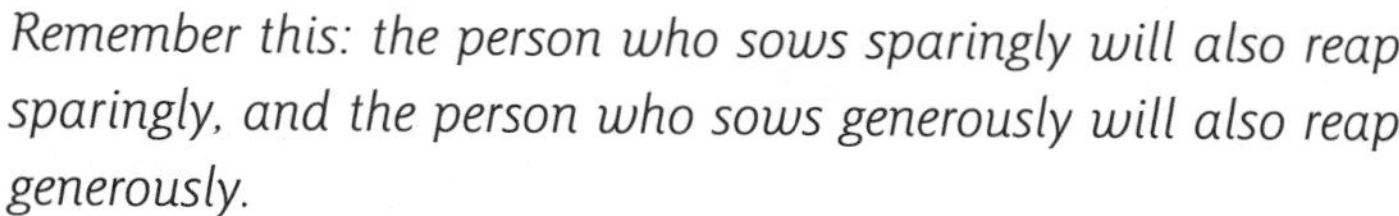

Remember this: the person who sows sparingly will also reap sparingly, and the person who sows generously will also reap generously.

2 Corinthians 9:6 Holman CSB

Jesus told us that we should be generous with other people, but sometimes we don't feel much like sharing. Instead of sharing the things that we have, we want to keep them all to ourselves. But God doesn't want selfishness to rule our hearts; He wants us to be generous.

Are you lucky enough to have nice things? If so, God's instructions are clear: you must share your blessings with others. And that's exactly the way it should be. After all, think how generous God has been with you.

Sleep On It!

There is a direct relationship between generosity and joy—the more you give to others, the more joy you will experience for yourself.

Bedtime Devotional 58

Never-Ending Love

The unfailing love of the Lord never ends!

Lamentations 3:22 NLT

How much does God love you? He loves you so much that He sent His Son Jesus to come to this earth for you! And, when you accept Jesus into your heart, God gives you a gift that is more precious than gold: that gift is called "eternal life," which means that you will live forever with God in heaven!

God's love is bigger and more powerful than anybody can imagine, but it is very real. So do yourself a favor right now: accept God's love with open arms and welcome His Son Jesus into your heart. When you do, your life will be changed today, tomorrow, and forever.

Sleep On It!

As God's children, we are the recipients of lavish love—a love that motivates us to keep trusting even when we have no idea what God is doing.

Beth Moore

Tonight, Here Are Some Big Ideas About Wisdom

Here are two important ideas. Take a few minutes to talk to your mom or dad about what these quotations mean.

If you lack knowledge, go to school.
If you lack wisdom, get on your knees.

Vance Havner

The theme of Proverbs is wisdom,
the right use of knowledge.
It enables you to evaluate circumstances
and people and make the right decisions in life.

Warren Wiersbe

Is the Golden Rule Your Rule, Too?

Don't be selfish . . . . Be humble, thinking of others as better than yourself.

Philippians 2:3 TLB

Is the Golden Rule your rule, or is it just another Bible verse that goes in one ear and out the other? Jesus made Himself perfectly clear: He instructed you to treat other people in the same way that you want to be treated. But sometimes, especially when you're feeling pressure from friends, or when you're tired or upset, obeying the Golden Rule can seem like an impossible task—but it's not. So be kind to everybody and obey God's rule, the Golden Rule, that is.

Sleep On It!

You must do more than talk about it. In order to be a good person, you must do good things. So get busy! The best time to do a good deed is as soon as you can do it!

Bedtime Devotional 61

The Habit of Honesty

Those who want to do right more than anything else are happy. God will fully satisfy them.

Matthew 5:6 ICB

Our lives are made up of lots and lots of habits. And the habits we choose help determine the kind of people we become. If we choose habits that are good, we are happier and healthier. If we choose habits that are bad, then it's too bad for us!

Honesty, like so many other things, is a habit. And it's a habit that is right for you.

Do you want to grow up to become the kind of man that God intends for you to be? Then get into the habit of being honest with everybody. You'll be glad you did . . . and so will God!

Sleep On It!

If you want to form a new habit, get to work. If you want to break a bad habit, get on your knees.

Marie T. Freeman

White Lies?

Doing what is right brings freedom to honest people.

Proverbs 11:6 ICB

Sometimes, people convince themselves that it's okay to tell "little white lies." Sometimes people convince themselves that itsy bitsy lies aren't harmful. But there's a problem: little lies have a way of growing into big ones, and once they grow up, they cause lots of problems.

Remember that lies, no matter what size, are not part of God's plan for our lives, so tell the truth about everything. It's the right thing to do, and besides: when you always tell the truth, you don't have to try and remember what you said!

Sleep On It!

The single most important element in any human relationship is honesty—with oneself, with God, and with others.

Catherine Marshall

Bedtime Devotional 63

A Fruitful Friendship

I am the Vine, you are the branches. When you're joined with me and I with you, the relation intimate and organic, the harvest is sure to be abundant.

John 15:5 MSG

Whether you realize it or not, you already have a relationship with Jesus. Hopefully, it's a close relationship! Why? Because the friendship you form with Jesus will help you every day of your life . . . and beyond!

You can either choose to invite Him into your heart, or you can ignore Him altogether. Welcome Him today—and while you're at it, encourage your friends and family members to do the same.

Sleep On It!

I am truly happy with Jesus Christ. I couldn't live without Him. When my life gets beyond the ability to cope, He takes over.

Ruth Bell Graham

Bedtime Devotional 64

Laughter Is a Gift

There is a time for everything, and everything on earth has its special season. There is a time to cry and a time to laugh. There is a time to be sad and a time to dance.

Ecclesiastes 3:1,4 NCV

Do you like to laugh? Of course you do! Laughter is a gift from God that He hopes you'll use in the right way. So here are a few things to remember:

1. God wants you to be happy. 2. Laughter is a good thing when you're laughing at the right things. 3. You should laugh with people, but you should never laugh at them.

God created laughter for a reason . . . and God knows best. So do yourself a favor: laugh at the right things . . . and laugh a lot!

Sleep On It!

Life has a lighter side—look for it, especially when times are tough. Laughter is medicine for the soul, so take your medicine early and often.

Bedtime Devotional 65

Tonight, Here Are Some Big Ideas About Going to Church

Here are two important ideas. Take a few minutes to talk to your mom or dad about what these quotations mean.

The church needs people who are doers
of the Word and not just hearers.

Warren Wiersbe

Christians are like coals in a fire.
Together they glow—apart they grow cold.

Anonymous

Obey Your Teachers

And the world with its lust is passing away, but the one who does God's will remains forever.

I John 2:17 Holman CSB

It's good to obey your teachers, but before you can obey them, you must make sure you understand what your teachers are saying. So, in order to be an obedient student, you must be a student who knows how to listen.

Once you decide to be a careful listener, you'll become a better learner, too. But if you're determined to talk to other kids while your teachers are teaching, you won't learn very much.

So do yourself a favor: when you go to school or church, listen and obey. You'll be glad you did. . . and your teachers will be glad, too.

Sleep On It!

You have many teachers. Listen to them and obey them. When you do, you'll become a better person.

Bedtime Devotional 67

Hopes, Hopes, and More Hopes

Make me hear joy and gladness.

Psalm 51:8 NKJV

Hope is a very good thing to have . . . and to share. So make this promise to yourself and keep it: promise yourself that you'll be a hopeful person. Think good thoughts. Trust God. Become friends with Jesus. And trust your hopes, not your fears. Then, when you've filled your heart with hope and gladness, share your good thoughts with friends. They'll be better for it, and so will you.

Sleep On It!

Think about all the things you have (starting with your family and your faith) . . . and think about all the things you can do! Believe in yourself.

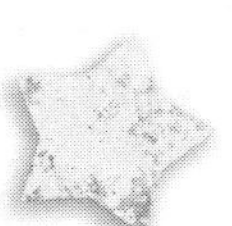

Bedtime Devotional 68

Be Respectful

Show respect for all people. Love the brothers and sisters of God's family.

1 Peter 2:17 ICB

Are you polite and respectful to your parents and teachers? And do you do your best to treat everybody with the respect they deserve? If you want to obey God's rules, then you should be able to answer yes to these questions.

Remember this: the Bible teaches you to be a respectful person—and if it's right there in the Bible, it's certainly the right thing to do!

Sleep On It!

If you're angry with your mom or your dad, don't blurt out something unkind. If you can't say anything nice, go to your room and don't come out until you can.

When Nobody Is Watching

Moderation is better than muscle, self-control better than political power.

Proverbs 16:32 MSG

When your teachers or parents aren't watching, what should you do? The answer, of course, is that you should behave exactly like you would if they were watching you. But sometimes, you may be tempted to do otherwise.

When a parent steps away or a teacher looks away, you may be tempted to say something or do something that you would not do if they were standing right beside you. But remember this: when nobody's watching, it's up to you to control yourself. And that's exactly what everybody wants you to do: your teachers want you to control yourself, and so do your parents. And so, by the way, does God.

Sleep On It!

God nowhere tells us to give up things for the sake of giving them up. He tells us to give them up for the sake of the only thing worth having—life with Himself.

Oswald Chambers

Bedtime Devotional 70

God Wants You to Share

I will make you into a great nation and I will bless you; I will make your name great, and you will be a blessing. I will bless those who bless you, and whoever curses you I will curse; and all peoples on earth will be blessed through you.

Genesis 12:2-3 NIV

You've heard it plenty of times from your parents and teachers: share your things. But it's important to realize that sharing isn't just something that grown-ups want you to do. It's also something that God wants you to do, too.

The word "possessions" is another way of describing the stuff that belongs to you: your clothes, your toys, your books, and things like that are "your possessions."

Jesus says that you should learn how to share your possessions without feeling bad about it. Sometimes, of course, it's very hard to share and very easy to be stingy. But God wants you to share—and to keep sharing! Since that's what God wants, it's what you should want, too.

Sleep On It!

Don't be afraid to share what you have with others; after all, it all belongs to God anyway.

Jim Gallery

Bedtime Devotional 71

Sharing Your Stuff

In every way I've shown you that by laboring like this, it is necessary to help the weak and to keep in mind the words of the Lord Jesus, for He said, "It is more blessed to give than to receive."

Acts 20:35 Holman CSB

Are you one of those boys who is lucky enough to have a closet filled up with stuff? If so, it's probably time to share some of it.

When your mom or dad says it's time to clean up your closet and give some things away, don't be sad. Instead of whining, think about all the children who could enjoy the things that you don't use very much. And while you're at it, think about what Jesus might tell you to do if He were here. Jesus would tell you to share generously and cheerfully. And that's exactly what you should do!

Sleep On It!

Finding loving homes for your old clothes and toys. Your parents can help you find younger children who need the clothes and toys that you've outgrown.

Bedtime Devotional 72

How Would He Behave?

And he saith unto them, follow me, and I will make you fishers of men. And they straightway left their nets, and followed him.

Matthew 4:19-20 KJV

If Jesus were here, how would He behave? He would be loving and forgiving. He would worship God with sincere devotion. He would serve other people, and He would always abide by the Golden Rule. If Jesus were here, He would stand up for truth and speak out against evil.

We read in the Bible that Jesus wants each of us to do our best to be like Him. We can't be perfect Christians, but we can do our best to obey God's commandments and to follow Christ's example. When we do so, we bring honor to the One who gave His life for each of us.

Sleep On It!

When you have an important decision to make, stop for a minute and think about how Jesus would behave if He were in your shoes.

Bedtime Devotional 73

A Pleasing Attitude

Set your minds on what is above, not on what is on the earth.

Colossians 3:2 Holman CSB

God knows everything about you, including your attitude. And when your attitude is good, God is pleased . . . very pleased.

Are you interested in pleasing God? Are you interested in pleasing your parents? Your teachers? And your friends? If so, try to make your attitude the best it can be. When you try hard to have a good attitude, you'll make other people feel better—and you'll make yourself feel better, too.

Sleep On It!

Remember that you can choose to have a good attitude or a not-so good attitude. And it's a choice you make every day.

Bedtime Devotional 74

Your Most Important Book

But grow in the grace and knowledge of our Lord and Savior Jesus Christ. To Him be the glory both now and forever. Amen.

2 Peter 3:18 NKJV

What book contains everything that God has to say about His rules and His Son? The Bible, of course. If you read the Bible every day, you'll soon learn how God wants you to behave.

Since doing the right thing (and the smart thing) is important to God, it should be important to you, too. And you'll learn what's right by reading the Bible.

The Bible is the most important book you'll ever own. It's God's Holy Word. Read it every day, and follow its instructions. When you do, you'll be safe now and forever.

Sleep On It!

Try to read your Bible with your parents every day. If they forget, remind them!

Bedtime Devotional 75

Your Continual Feast

A cheerful heart has a continual feast.

Proverbs 15:15 Holman CSB

What is a continual feast? It's a little bit like a non-stop birthday party: fun, fun, and more fun! The Bible tells us that a cheerful heart can make life like a continual feast, and that's something worth working for.

Where does cheerfulness begin? It begins inside each of us; it begins in the heart. So please be thankful to God for His blessings, and let's show our thanks by sharing good cheer wherever we go. This old world needs all the cheering up it can get . . . and so do we!

Sleep On It!

When we bring sunshine into the lives of others, we're warmed by it ourselves. When we spill a little happiness, it splashes on us.

Barbara Johnson

Bedtime Devotional 76

Slowing Down for God!

Don't burn out; keep yourselves fueled and aflame. Be alert servants of the Master, cheerfully expectant. Don't quit in hard times; pray all the harder.

Romans 12:11-12 MSG

Everybody knows you're a very busy boy. But here's a question: are you able to squeeze time into your schedule for God? Hopefully so!

Nothing is more important than the time you spend with your Heavenly Father. So take some time tonight and every night to pray and to thank God for His blessings. God will be glad you did, and you'll be glad, too.

Sleep On It!

We often become mentally and spiritually worn out because we're so busy.

Franklin Graham

Making Things Better

For out of the overflow of the heart the mouth speaks.

Matthew 12:34 NIV

When we're frustrated or tired, it's easier to speak first and think second. But that's not the best way to talk to other people. The Bible tells us that "a good person's words will help many others." But if our words are to be helpful, we must put some thought into them.

The next time you're tempted to say something unkind, remember that your words can and should be helpful to others, not hurtful. God wants to use you to make this world a better place, and He will use the things that you say to help accomplish that goal . . . if you let Him.

Sleep On It!

Words have the power to encourage or discourage others. So watch what you say.

Bedtime Devotional 78

Tonight, Try to Memorize This Verse

For to me to live is Christ,
and to die is gain.

Philippians 1:21 KJV

This is an important Bible verse. Practice saying it several times. And then, talk to your mom or dad about exactly what the verse means . . .

A Tip for Parents

Tonight, talk to your child about . . .
living for Christ.

Bedtime Devotional 79

What Kind of Example?

You are young, but do not let anyone treat you as if you were not important. Be an example to show the believers how they should live. Show them with your words, with the way you live, with your love, with your faith, and with your pure life.

I Timothy 4:12 ICB

Like it or not, your behavior is a powerful example to others. The question is not whether you will be an example to your friends; the only question is this: What kind of example will you be?

Corrie ten Boom advised, "Don't worry about what you do not understand. Worry about what you do understand in the Bible but do not live by." And that's good advice because your family and friends are always watching . . . and so, for that matter, is God.

Sleep On It!

Don't exaggerate! All of us have enough troubles without pretending that we have more.

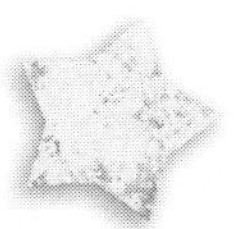

Bedtime Devotional 80

Obeying God

Be gentle with one another, sensitive. Forgive one another as quickly and thoroughly as God in Christ forgave you.

Ephesians 4:32 MSG

How hard is it to forgive people? Sometimes, it's very hard! But God tells us that we must forgive other people, even when we'd rather not forgive them. So, if you're angry with anybody (or if you're upset by something you yourself have done) it's time to forgive.

God instructs us to treat other people exactly as we wish to be treated. When we forgive others, we are obeying our Heavenly Father, and that's exactly what we must try to do.

Sleep On It!

Forgiving other people is not necessarily the same as forgetting. Yet even when you cannot forget the past, you should try not to focus on the past.

Bedtime Devotional 81

Real Friends

A friend loves you all the time.

Proverbs 17:17 ICB

The Book of Proverbs tells us that true friends love us always. How wonderful that is! We should thank God for the family and friends He has brought into our lives.

Today, let's give thanks to God for all the people who love us, for brothers and sisters, parents and grandparents, aunts and uncles, cousins, and friends. And then, as a way of thanking God, let's obey Him by being especially kind to our loved ones. They deserve it, and so does He.

Sleep On It!

To grow your friendships, make the effort to spend time with your friends.

Bedtime Devotional 82

Sharing and Self-esteem

God loves the person who gives happily.

2 Corinthians 9:7 ICB

Learning how to share can be an important way to build better self-esteem. Why? Because when you learn to share your things, you'll know that you've done exactly what God wants you to do—and you'll feel better about yourself.

The Bible teaches that it's better to be generous than selfish. But sometimes, you won't feel like sharing your things, and you'll be tempted to keep everything for yourself. When you're feeling a little bit stingy, remember this: God wants you to share your things with people who need your help.

When you learn to be a more generous boy, God will be pleased with you . . . and you'll be pleased with yourself.

Sleep On It!

Some of the best stuff you'll ever have is the stuff you give away.

Bedtime Devotional 83

Tonight, Here Are Some Big Ideas About God's Gifts

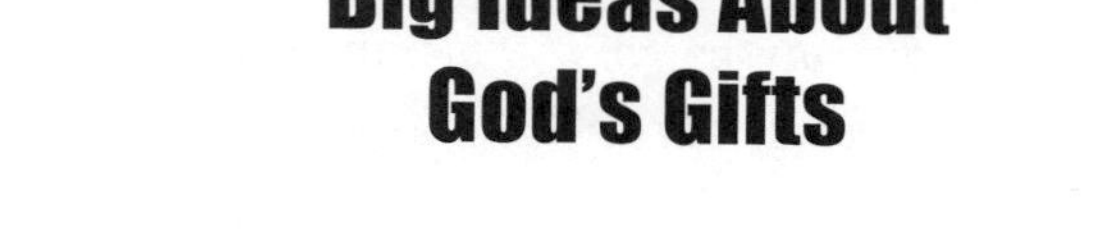

Here are two important ideas. Take a few minutes to talk to your mom or dad about what these quotations mean.

God never turns away from the sincere heart.

Max Lucado

God is the giver, and we are the receivers.
And His richest gifts are bestowed not upon those
who do the greatest things, but upon those who accept
His abundance and His grace.

Hannah Whitall Smith

God's Power

I pray . . . that you may know . . . his uncomparably great power for us who believe . . . .

Ephesians 1:18-19 NIV

How strong is God? Stronger than anybody can imagine! But even if we can't understand God's power, we can respect His power. And we can be sure that God has the strength to guide us and protect us forever.

The next time you're worried or afraid, remember this: if God is powerful enough to create the universe and everything in it, He's also strong enough to take care of you. Now that's a comforting thought!

Sleep On It!

The power of God through His Spirit will work within us to the degree that we permit it.

Mrs. Charles E. Cowman

Bedtime Devotional 85

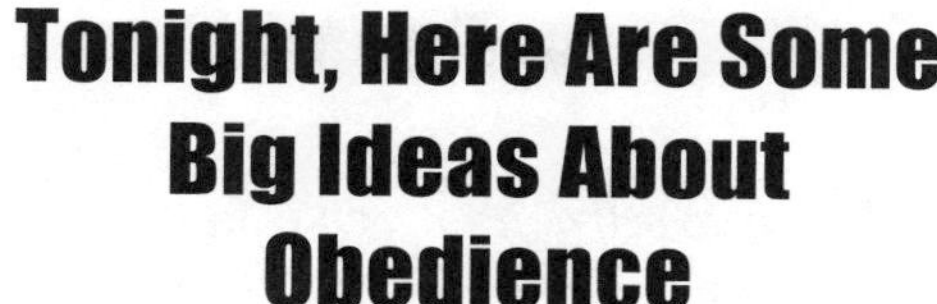

Here are two important ideas. Take a few minutes to talk to your mom or dad about what these quotations mean.

> You may not always see immediate results,
> but all God wants is your obedience and faithfulness.
>
> Vonette Bright

> The surest evidence of our love to Christ
> is obedience to the laws of Christ.
> Love is the root, obedience is the fruit.
>
> Matthew Henry

Bedtime Devotional 86

Slow Down!

Knowing God leads to self-control. Self-control leads to patient endurance, and patient endurance leads to godliness.

2 Peter 1:6 NLT

Maybe you're one of those boys who try to do everything fast, faster, or fastest! If so, maybe you sometimes do things before you think about the consequences of your actions. If that's the case, it's probably a good idea to slow down a little bit so you can think before you act. When you do, you'll soon discover the value of thinking carefully about things before you get started. And while you're at it, it's probably a good idea to think before you speak, too. After all, you'll never have to apologize for something that you didn't say.

Sleep On It!

Discipline is training that develops and corrects.

Charles Stanley

Bedtime Devotional 87

Sharing

If you have two shirts, share with the person who does not have one. If you have food, share that too.

Luke 3:11 ICB

How many times have you heard someone say, "Don't touch that; it's mine!" If you're like most of us, you've heard those words many times and you may have even said them yourself.

The Bible tells us that it's better for us to share things than it is to keep them all to ourselves. And the Bible also tells us that when we share, it's best to do so cheerfully. So be sure to share. It's the best way because it's God's way.

Sleep On It!

Your acts of kindness and generosity will speak far louder than words.

Bedtime Devotional 88

The Words You Speak

If anyone considers himself religious and yet does not keep a tight rein on his tongue, he deceives himself and his religion is worthless.

James 1:26 NIV

The words you speak are important. If you speak kind words, you make other people feel better. And that's exactly what you should do!

How hard is it to say a kind word? Not very! Yet sometimes we're so busy that we forget to say the very things that might make other people feel better.

Kind words help; cruel words hurt. It's as simple as that. And, when we say the right thing at the right time, we give a gift that can change somebody's day or somebody's life.

Sleep On It!

If you're not sure that it's the right thing to say, don't say it! And if you're not sure that it's the truth, don't tell it.

Tonight, Try to Memorize This Verse

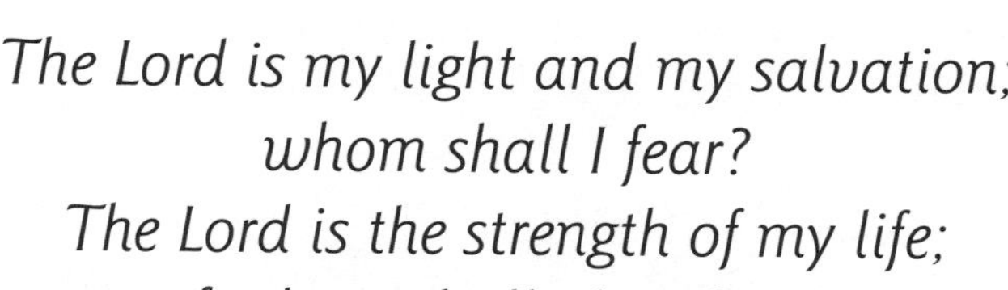

The Lord is my light and my salvation;
whom shall I fear?
The Lord is the strength of my life;
of whom shall I be afraid?

Psalm 27:1 KJV

This is an important Bible verse. Practice saying it several times. And then, talk to your mom or dad about exactly what the verse means . . .

A Tip for Parents

Tonight, talk to your child about . . .
God's protection.

Bedtime Devotional 90

Everlasting Protection

The Lord is my rock, my fortress, and my deliverer, my God, my mountain where I seek refuge. My shield, the horn of my salvation, my stronghold, my refuge, and my Savior.

2 Samuel 22:2-3 Holman CSB

Life isn't always easy. Far from it! Sometimes, life can be very hard indeed. But even when we're upset or hurt, we must remember that we're protected by a loving Heavenly Father.

When we're worried, God can reassure us; when we're sad, God can comfort us. When our feelings are hurt, God is not just near, He is here. We must lift our thoughts and prayers to our Father in heaven. When we do, He will answer our prayers. Why? Because He is our shepherd, and He has promised to protect us now and forever.

Sleep On It!

The best protection comes from the loving heart of God—and from the salvation that flows from His only begotten Son.

No More Tantrums

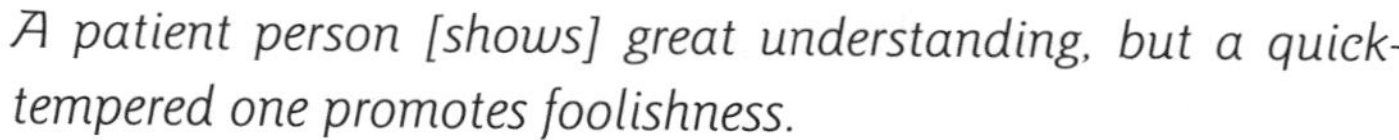

A patient person [shows] great understanding, but a quick-tempered one promotes foolishness.

Proverbs 14:29 Holman CSB

Temper tantrums are so silly. And so is pouting. So, of course, is whining. When we lose our tempers, we say things that we shouldn't say, and we do things that we shouldn't do. Too bad!

The Bible tells us that it is foolish to become angry and that it is wise to remain calm. That's why we should learn to control our tempers before our tempers control us.

Sleep On It!

If you think you're about to pitch a fit or throw a tantrum, slow down, catch your breath, and walk away if you must. It's better to walk away—and keep walking—than it is to blurt out angry words that can't be un-blurted.

Bedtime Devotional 92

Patience and Love

I wait for the Lord; I wait, and put my hope in His word.

Psalm 130:5 Holman CSB

God has a perfect idea of the kind of people He wants us to become. And for starters, He wants us to be loving, kind, and patient—not rude or mean!

The Bible tells us that God is love and that if we wish to know Him, we must have love in our hearts. Sometimes, of course, when we're tired, angry, or frustrated, it is very hard for us to be loving. Thankfully, anger and frustration are feelings that come and go, but God's love lasts forever.

If you'd like to become a more patient boy, talk to God in prayer, listen to what He says, and share His love with your family and friends. God is always listening, and He's ready to talk to you . . . now!

Sleep On It!

God has been patient with you . . . now it's your turn to be patient with others.

Bedtime Devotional 93

Know When to Say No

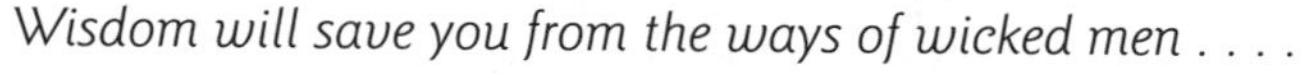

Wisdom will save you from the ways of wicked men . . . .

Proverbs 2:12 NIV

It happens to all of us at one time or another: a friend asks us to do something that we think is wrong. What should we do? Should we try to please our friend by doing something bad? No way! It's not worth it!

Trying to please our friends is okay. What's not okay is misbehaving in order to do so. Do you have a friend who encourages you to misbehave? Hopefully you don't have any friends like that. But if you do, say "No, NO, NOOOOOO!" And what if your friend threatens to break up the friendship? Let him! Friendships like that just aren't worth it.

Sleep On It!

You will get untold flak for prioritizing God's revealed and present will for your life over man's . . . but, boy, is it worth it.

Beth Moore

Tonight, Here Are Some Big Ideas About Cheerfulness

Here are two important ideas. Take a few minutes to talk to your mom or dad about what these quotations mean.

> When we bring sunshine into the lives of others,
> we're warmed by it ourselves.
> When we spill a little happiness, it splashes on us.
>
> Barbara Johnson

> We may run, walk, stumble, drive, or fly,
> but let us never lose sight of the reason for the journey,
> or miss a chance to see a rainbow on the way.
>
> Gloria Gaither

Bedtime Devotional 95

He Answers

For I know the thoughts that I think toward you, says the Lord, thoughts of peace and not of evil, to give you a future and a hope. Then you will call upon Me and go and pray to Me, and I will listen to you.

Jeremiah 29:11-12 NKJV

In case you've been wondering, wonder no more—God does answer your prayers. What God does not do is this: He does not always answer your prayers as soon as you might like, and He does not always answer your prayers by saying "Yes."

God answers prayers not only according to our wishes but also according to His master plan. And guess what? We don't know that plan . . . but we can know the Planner.

Are you praying? Then you can be sure that God is listening. And sometime soon, He'll answer!

Sleep On It!

You don't need fancy words or religious phrases. Just tell God the way it really is.

Jim Cymbala

Bedtime Devotional 96

Respect for Others

Being respected is more important than having great riches.

Proverbs 22:1 ICB

Do you try to have a respectful attitude towards everybody? Hopefully so!

Should you be respectful of grown ups? Of course. Teachers? Certainly. Family members? Yes. Friends? Yep, but it doesn't stop there. The Bible teaches us to treat all people with respect.

Respect for others is habit-forming: the more you do it, the easier it becomes. So start practicing right now. Say lots of kind words and do lots of kind things, because when it comes to kindness and respect, practice makes perfect.

Sleep On It!

How did Jesus treat the poor people? And how did He treat people who lived on the edges of society? With patience, respect, and love.

Bedtime Devotional 97

Do Good Deeds

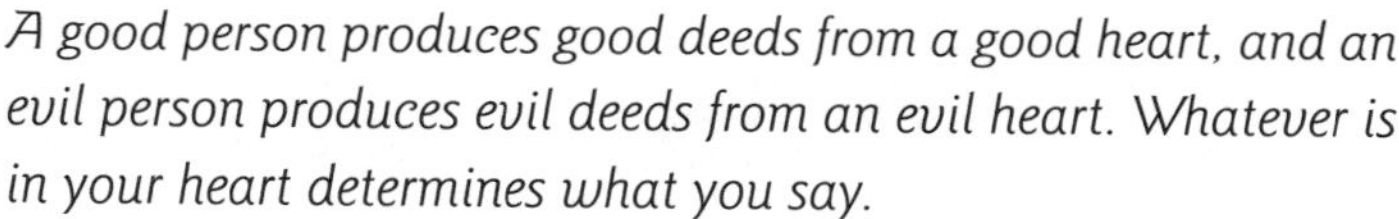

A good person produces good deeds from a good heart, and an evil person produces evil deeds from an evil heart. Whatever is in your heart determines what you say.

Luke 6:45 NLT

It's good to do good deeds. Even when nobody's watching, God is. And God knows whether you've done the right thing or the wrong thing.

So if you're tempted to misbehave when nobody is looking, remember this: There is never a time when "nobody's watching." Somebody is always watching over you—and that Somebody, of course, is your Father in heaven. Don't let Him down!

Sleep On It!

Goodness is as goodness does: In order to be a good person, you must do good things. Thinking about them isn't enough. So get busy! Your family and friends need all the good deeds they can get!

Bedtime Devotional 98

Sometimes It's Hard to Be Honest, But It's Always Right

It is better to be poor and honest than to be foolish and tell lies.

Proverbs 19:1 ICB

Telling the truth can be hard sometimes. But even when telling the truth is very hard, that's exactly what you should do. If you're afraid to tell the truth, pray to God for the courage to do the right thing, and then do it!

If you've ever told a big lie, and then had to live with the big consequences of that lie, you know that it's far more trouble to tell a lie than it is to tell the truth. But lies aren't just troubling to us; they're also troubling to God! So tell the truth, even when it's hard to do; you'll be glad you did . . . and so will He!

Sleep On It!

Honesty has a beautiful and refreshing simplicity about it. No hidden meanings. As honesty and integrity characterize our lives, there will be no need to manipulate others.

Charles Swindoll

Bedtime Devotional 99

The Master Teacher

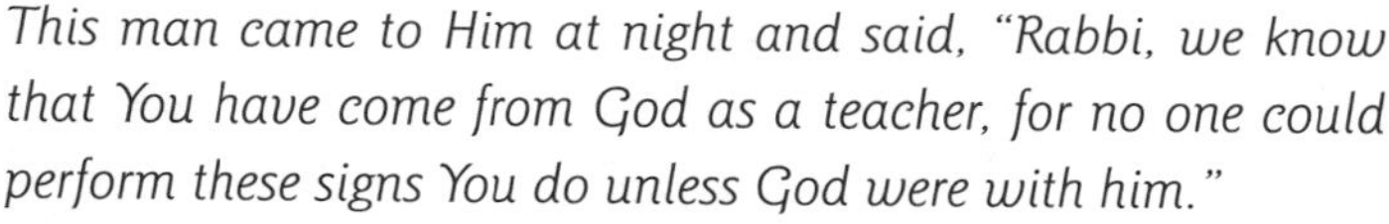

This man came to Him at night and said, "Rabbi, we know that You have come from God as a teacher, for no one could perform these signs You do unless God were with him."

John 3:2 Holman CSB

Who was the greatest teacher in the history of the world? Jesus was . . and He still is! Jesus teaches us how to live, how to behave, and how to worship. Now, it's up to each of us, as Christians, to learn the important lessons that Jesus can teach.

Some day soon, you will have learned everything that Jesus has to teach you, right? WRONG!!!! Jesus will keep teaching you important lessons throughout your life. And that's good, because all of us, kids and grown-ups alike, have lots to learn . . . especially from the Master . . . and the Master, of course, is Jesus.

Sleep On It!

The Truth with a capital "T": Jesus is the Truth, and that's the truth!

It's Important to Be Kind

I tell you the truth, anything you did for even the least of my people here, you also did for me.

Matthew 25:40 NCV

The Bible promises that if you're a nice person, good things will happen to you. That's one reason (but not the only reason) that it's important to be kind.

Do you listen to your heart when it tells you to be kind to other people? Hopefully, you do. After all, lots of people in the world aren't as fortunate as you are—and some of these folks are living very near you.

Ask your parents to help you find ways to do nice things for other people. And don't forget that everybody needs love, kindness, and respect, so you should always be ready to share those things, too.

Sleep On It!

When you extend hospitality to others, you're not trying to impress people, you're trying to reflect God to them.

Max Lucado

Tonight, Here Are Some Big Ideas About Too Much Stuff

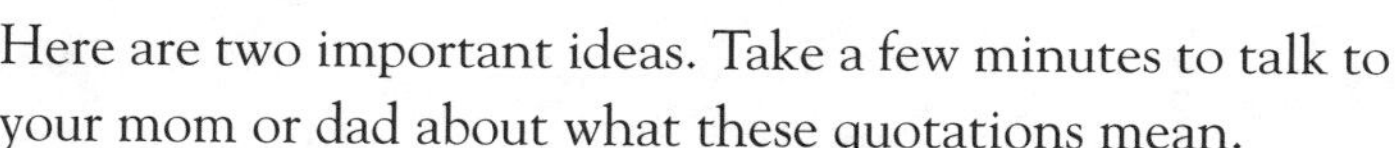

Here are two important ideas. Take a few minutes to talk to your mom or dad about what these quotations mean.

> If you want to be truly happy, you won't find it on an endless quest for more stuff. You'll find it in receiving God's generosity and then passing that generosity along.
>
> Bill Hybels

> There is absolutely no evidence that complexity and materialism lead to happiness. On the contrary, there is plenty of evidence that simplicity and spirituality lead to joy, a blessedness that is better than happiness.
>
> Dennis Swanberg

Nobody Likes 'Em

Therefore, if anyone is in Christ, he is a new creation; the old has gone, the new has come!

2 Corinthians 5:17 NIV

Mistakes: nobody likes 'em but everybody makes 'em. And you're no different! When you make mistakes (and you will), you should do your best to correct them, to learn from them, and pray for the wisdom to avoid those same mistakes in the future.

If you want to become smarter faster, you'll learn from your mistakes the first time you make them. When you do, that means that you won't keep making the same mistakes over and over again, and that's the smart way to live.

Sleep On It!

Made a mistake? Ask for forgiveness! If you've broken one of God's rules, you can always ask Him for His forgiveness. And He will always give it!

Bedtime Devotional 103

Parents Can Help

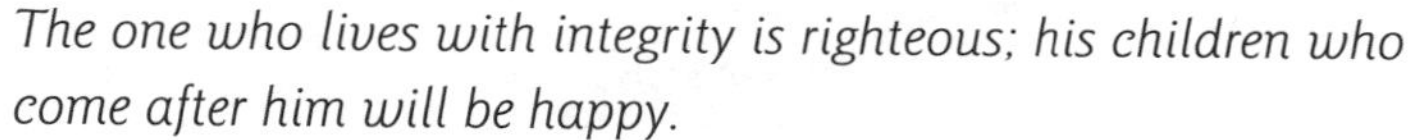

The one who lives with integrity is righteous; his children who come after him will be happy.

Proverbs 20:7 Holman CSB

Whenever you want to get better at something, you should always be willing to let your parents help out in any way they can. After all, your parents want you to become the very best person you can be. So, if you want to become better at controlling your own behavior, ask your parents to help. How can they help out? By reminding you to slow down and think about things before you do them—not after. It's as simple as that.

Sleep On It!

Your parents love you and want to help you. Their job is to help . . . your job is to listen carefully to the things they say.

Tonight, Here Are Some Big Ideas About Heaven

Here are two important ideas. Take a few minutes to talk to your mom or dad about what these quotations mean.

What joy that the Bible tells us the great comfort
that the best is yet to be.
Our outlook goes beyond this world.

Corrie ten Boom

Earth's best is only a dim reflection and a preliminary
rendering of the glory that will one day be revealed.

Joni Eareckson Tada

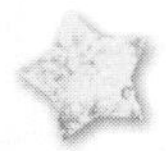

Bedtime Devotional 105

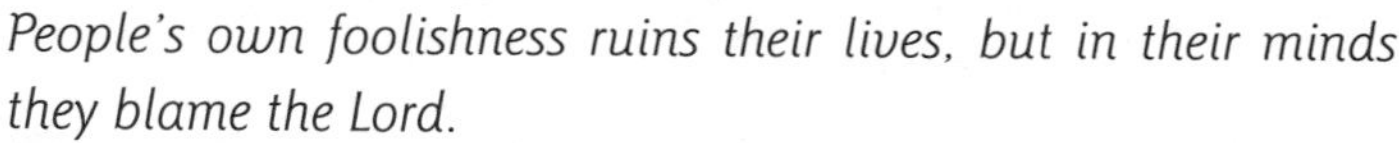

The Blame Game

People's own foolishness ruins their lives, but in their minds they blame the Lord.

Proverbs 19:3 NCV

When something goes wrong, do you look for somebody to blame? And do you try to blame other people even if you're the one who made the mistake? Hopefully not!

It's silly to try to blame other people for your own mistakes, so don't do it.

If you've done something you're ashamed of, don't look for somebody to blame; look for a way to say, "I'm sorry, and I won't make that same mistake again."

Sleep On It!

It's very tempting to blame others when you make a mistake, but it's more honest to look in the mirror first.

Bedtime Devotional 106

What Your Conscience Says About Forgiveness

Now the goal of our instruction is love from a pure heart, a good conscience, and a sincere faith.

I Timothy 1:5 Holman CSB

God gave you something called a conscience: it's that little feeling that tells you whether something is right or wrong. Your conscience will usually tell you what to do and when to do it. Trust that feeling.

If you listen to your conscience, it won't be as hard for you to forgive people. Why? Because forgiving other people is the right thing to do. And, it's what God wants you to do. And it's what your conscience tells you to do. So what are you waiting for?

Sleep On It!

Trust the quiet inner voice of your conscience: Treat your conscience as you would a trusted advisor.

When People Are Cruel

A kind man benefits himself, but a cruel man brings disaster on himself.

Proverbs 11:17 Holman CSB

Face it: sometimes people can be cruel. And when people are unkind to you or to your friends, you may be tempted to strike back in anger. Don't do it! Instead, remember that God corrects other people's behaviors in His own way, and He doesn't need your help. So even when other people misbehave, God wants you to forgive them . . . and that's what you should do.

Sleep On It!

Do you know children who say or do cruel things to other kids? If so, don't join in! Instead, stand up for those who need your help. It's the right thing to do.

Positive Peer Pressure

My dear, dear friends, if God loved us like this, we certainly ought to love each other.

I John 4:11 MSG

Are your friends the kind of kids who encourage you to behave yourself? If so, you've chosen your friends wisely.

But if your friends try to get you in trouble, perhaps it's time to think long and hard about making some new friends.

Whether you know it or not, you're probably going to behave like your friends behave. So pick out friends who make you want to behave better, not worse. When you do, you'll be saving yourself from a lot of trouble . . . a whole lot of trouble.

Sleep On It!

Choose wise friends, and listen carefully to the things they say.

Bedtime Devotional 109

How Do They Know?

Do you want to be counted wise, to build a reputation for wisdom? Here's what you do: Live well, live wisely, live humbly. It's the way you live, not the way you talk, that counts.

James 3:13 MSG

How do people know that you're a Christian? Well, you can tell them, of course. And make no mistake about it: talking about your faith in God is a very good thing to do. But simply telling people about Jesus isn't enough. You must also be willing to show people how a real Christian (like you) should behave. Does that sound like a big responsibility? It is . . . but you can do it!

Sleep On It!

The life you live is your most important testimony.

Bedtime Devotional 110

Willing to Forgive

Talk and act like a person expecting to be judged by the Rule that sets us free. For if you refuse to act kindly, you can hardly expect to be treated kindly. Kind mercy wins over harsh judgment every time.

James 2:12-13 MSG

The Bible tells us this: When other people do things that are wrong, we should forgive them. God's Word also tells us that when we're willing to forgive others, God is quick to forgive us for the mistakes that we make.

Has somebody done something that makes you angry? Talk things over with your mom or dad, and then be ready to forgive the person who has hurt your feelings. And remember: God wants you to hurry up and forgive others, just like God is always in a hurry to forgive you.

Sleep On It!

If forgiveness were easy, everybody would be doing it—but it's not always easy to forgive and forget. If you simply can't seem to forgive somebody, pray about it . . . and keep praying about it . . . until God helps you do the right thing.

Bedtime Devotional 111

Good and Evil

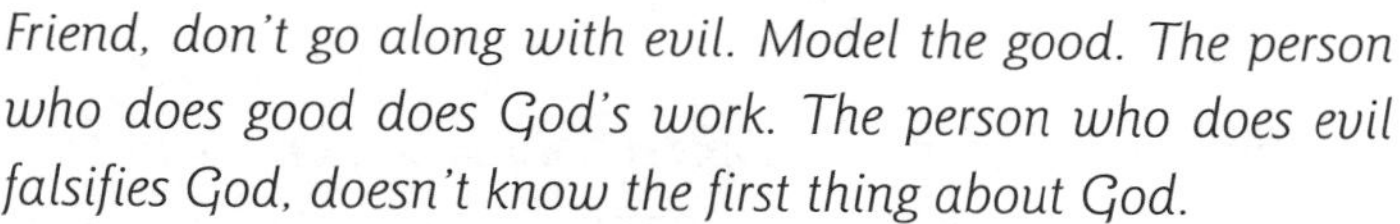

Friend, don't go along with evil. Model the good. The person who does good does God's work. The person who does evil falsifies God, doesn't know the first thing about God.

3 John 1:11 MSG

When other people are unkind, you may be tempted to strike back in anger. But God doesn't want you to fight your way through life! God wants you to forgive other people, even when they haven't behaved themselves, even when they've been very mean. So, when other people aren't nice, forgive them as quickly as you can. And let God take care of everything else.

Sleep On It!

God shapes the world by prayer. The more praying there is in the world, the better the world will be, and the mightier will be the forces against evil.

E. M. Bounds

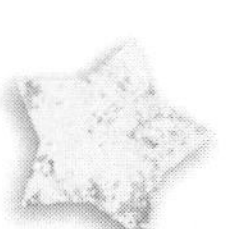

Being a Good Example to Your Friends

We have around us many people whose lives tell us what faith means. So let us run the race that is before us and never give up. We should remove from our lives anything that would get in the way and the sin that so easily holds us back.

Hebrews 12:1 NCV

Are you a boy whose behavior serves as a good example for other kids? If so, congratulations! God smiles upon people (like you) who do what's right, but that's not all. God also rewards good behavior when He sees it (and you can be sure that He sees it!).

So do yourself and your friends a favor: Do the right thing every chance you get.

Sleep On It!

The best example is Jesus. If you're not sure what to do, ask yourself what He would do.

Bedtime Devotional 113

Forgive and Forget

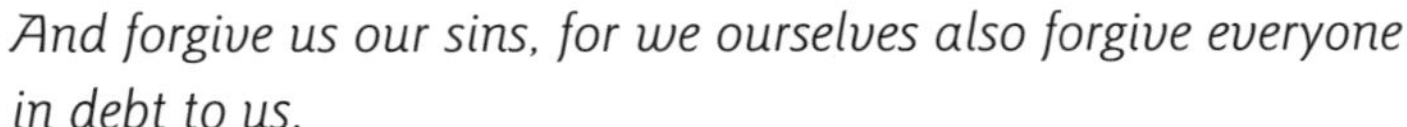

And forgive us our sins, for we ourselves also forgive everyone in debt to us.

Luke 11:4 Holman CSB

Have you heard the saying, "Forgive and forget"? Well, it's certainly easier said than done. It's easy to talk about forgiving somebody, but actually forgiving that person can be much harder to do. And when it comes to forgetting, forget about it!

Sometimes, it's impossible to forget the people who hurt our feelings. But even if we can't forget, we can forgive. And that's exactly what God teaches us to do.

Sleep On It!

Forgive . . . and keep forgiving! Sometimes, you may forgive someone once and then, at a later time, become angry at the very same person again. If so, you must forgive that person again and again . . . until it sticks!

Bedtime Devotional 114

Good Friends Behave

As iron sharpens iron, so people can improve each other.

Proverbs 27:17 NCV

Our world is filled with pressures: some good, some bad. The pressures that we feel to follow God's rules are the good kind of pressures (and the friends who make us want to obey God are good friends). But sometimes, we may feel pressure to misbehave, pressure from friends who want us to disobey the rules.

If you want to please God and your parents, make friends with people who behave themselves. When you do, you'll be much more likely to behave yourself, too . . . and that's a very good thing.

Sleep On It!

If you choose friends who behave themselves . . . you'll be far more likely to behave yourself, too.

You Can't Please Everybody

My son, if sinners entice you, don't be persuaded.

Proverbs 1:10 Holman CSB

Are you one of those boys who tries to please everybody in sight? If so, you'd better watch out! After all, if you worry too much about pleasing your friends, you may not worry enough about pleasing God.

Whom will you try to please today: your God or your pals? The answer to that question should be simple. Your first job is to obey God's rules . . . and that means obeying your parents, too!

So don't worry too much about pleasing your friends or neighbors. Try, instead, to please your Heavenly Father and your parents. No exceptions.

Sleep On It!

You simply cannot please everybody. So here's what you should do: Try pleasing God and your parents.

Bedtime Devotional 116

Practicing Forgiveness

Smart people know how to hold their tongue; their grandeur is to forgive and forget.

Proverbs 19:11 MSG

Forgiving other people requires practice and lots of it. So when it comes to forgiveness, here's something you should remember: if at first you don't succeed, don't give up!

Are you having trouble forgiving someone (or, for that matter, forgiving yourself for a mistake that you've made)? If so, remember that forgiveness isn't easy, so keep trying until you get it right . . . and if you keep trying, you can be sure that sooner or later, you will get it right.

Sleep On It!

For most of us—kids and grown-ups alike—forgiveness doesn't come naturally. Keep practicing until it does.

Bedtime Devotional 117

Tonight, Try to Memorize This Verse

For where two or three are
gathered together in My name,
I am there among them.

Matthew 18:20 Holman CSB

This is an important Bible verse. Practice saying it several times. And then, talk to your mom or dad about exactly what the verse means . . .

A Tip for Parents

Tonight, talk to your child about . . .
the presence of God.

Be the Right Kind of Christian

The one who plants and the one who waters have the same purpose, and each will be rewarded for his own work.

I Corinthians 3:8 NCV

Do you want to be the kind of Christian that God intends for you to be? It's up to you! You'll be the one who will decide how you behave.

If you decide to obey God and trust His Son, you will be rewarded now and forever. So guard your heart and trust your Heavenly Father. He will never lead you astray.

Sleep On It!

It's easy to blame others when you get into trouble . . . but it's wrong. Instead of trying to blame other people for your own misbehavior, take responsibility . . . and learn from your mistakes!

Bedtime Devotional 119

Tonight, Try to Memorize This Verse

Finishing is better
than starting.
Patience is better
than pride.

Ecclesiastes 7:8 NLT

This is an important Bible verse. Practice saying it several times. And then, talk to your mom or dad about exactly what the verse means . . .

A Tip for Parents

Tonight, talk to your child about . . .
perseverance and being patient.

Bedtime Devotional 120

Love Yourself, Too!

God began doing a good work in you, and I am sure he will continue it until it is finished when Jesus Christ comes again.

Philippians 1:6 NCV

The Bible teaches you this lesson: you should love everybody—and the word "everybody" includes yourself. Do you treat yourself with honor and respect? You should. After all, God created you in a very special way, and He loves you very much. And if God thinks you are amazing and wonderful, shouldn't you think about yourself in the same way? Of course you should!

So remember this: God wants you to love everybody, including the person you see when you look in the mirror. And one more thing: when you learn how to respect the person in the mirror, you'll be better at respecting other people, too.

Sleep On It!

When you learn about the Bible, you'll learn how much God loves you.

Bedtime Devotional 121

Learning How to Share

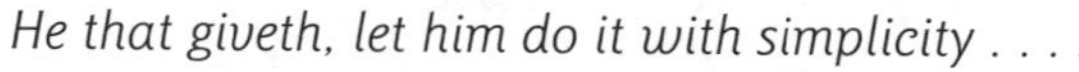

He that giveth, let him do it with simplicity . . . .

Romans 12:8 KJV

If you're having a little trouble learning how to share your stuff, you're not alone! Most people have problems letting go of things, so don't be discouraged. Just remember that learning to share requires practice and lots of it. The more you share—and the more you learn how good it feels to share—the sooner you'll be able to please God with the generosity and love that flows from your heart.

Sleep On It!

The mind grows by taking in, but the heart grows by giving out.

Warren Wiersbe

Bedtime Devotional 122

Tonight, Here Are Some Big Ideas About Respecting Other People

Here are two important ideas. Take a few minutes to talk to your mom or dad about what these quotations mean.

If you are willing to honor a person out of respect for God, you can be assured that God will honor you.

Beth Moore

Don't be a half-Christian. There are too many of them in the world already. The world has a profound respect for a person who is sincere in his faith.

Billy Graham

Bedtime Devotional 123

Sharing Is Better Than Stingy

And God will generously provide all you need. Then you will always have everything you need and plenty left over to share with others.

2 Corinthians 9:8 NLT

The Bible teaches that it's better to be generous than selfish. But sometimes, you won't feel like sharing your things, and you'll be tempted to keep everything for yourself. When you're feeling a little bit stingy, remember this: God wants you to share your things, and He will reward you when you do so.

When you learn to be a more generous person, God will be pleased with you . . . and you'll be pleased with yourself. So do yourself (and everybody else) a favor: be a little more generous, starting NOW!

Sleep On It!

When you are generous with others, God blesses you even more.

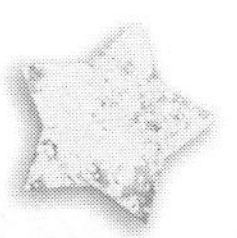

Bedtime Devotional 124

Tonight, Here Are Some Big Ideas About The Things You See on TV

Here are two important ideas. Take a few minutes to talk to your mom or dad about what these quotations mean.

If you give the devil an inch, he'll be a ruler.

Anonymous

The popular media has a way of attacking your senses and your heart. So be careful what you watch.

Criswell Freeman

Bedtime Devotional 125

Peace at Home

My dear brothers, always be willing to listen and slow to speak. Do not become angry easily. Anger will not help you live a good life as God wants.

James 1:19 ICB

Sometimes, it's easy to become angry with the people we love most, and sometimes it's hard to forgive them. After all, we know that our family will still love us no matter how angry we become. But while it's easy to become angry at home, it's usually wrong.

The next time you're tempted to stay angry at a brother, or a sister, or a parent, remember that these are the people who love you more than anybody else! Then, calm down, and forgive them . . . NOW! Because peace is always beautiful, especially when it's peace at your house.

Sleep On It!

When you strike out in anger, you may miss the other person, but you will always hit yourself.

Jim Gallery

Make Them Proud

Give generously, for your gifts will return to you later.

Ecclesiastes 11:1 NLT

It's tempting to be selfish, but it's wrong. It's tempting to want to keep everything for yourself, but it's better to share. It's tempting to say, "No, that's MINE!" but it's better to say, "I'll share it with you."

Are you sometimes tempted to be a little stingy? Are you sometimes tempted to say, "No, I don't want to share that!"—and then do you feel a little sorry that you said it? If that describes you, don't worry: everybody is tempted to be a little bit selfish. Your job is to remember this: even when it's tempting to be selfish, you should try very hard not to be. Because when you're generous, not selfish, you'll make your parents proud and you'll make your Father in heaven proud, too.

Sleep On It!

Would you like to be a little happier? The Bible says that if you become a more generous person, you'll become a happier person, too.

Tonight, Here Are Some Big Ideas About God's Protection

Here are two important ideas. Take a few minutes to talk to your mom or dad about what these quotations mean.

Under heaven's lock and key, we are protected by the most efficient security system available: the power of God.

Charles Swindoll

Prayer is our pathway not only to divine protection, but also to a personal, intimate relationship with God.

Shirley Dobson

Bedtime Devotional 128

God Is Close-by

Fear not, for I am with you; Be not dismayed, for I am your God. I will strengthen you.

Isaiah 41:10 NKJV

Here's a promise you can depend on: wherever you are, God is always there, too.

God doesn't take vacations, and He doesn't play hide-and-seek. He's always "right here, right now," waiting to hear from you. So if you're wondering where God is, wonder no more. He's here. And that's a promise!

Sleep On It!

God's presence provides comfort. Seek Him often and pray often.

You'll Feel Better About Yourself

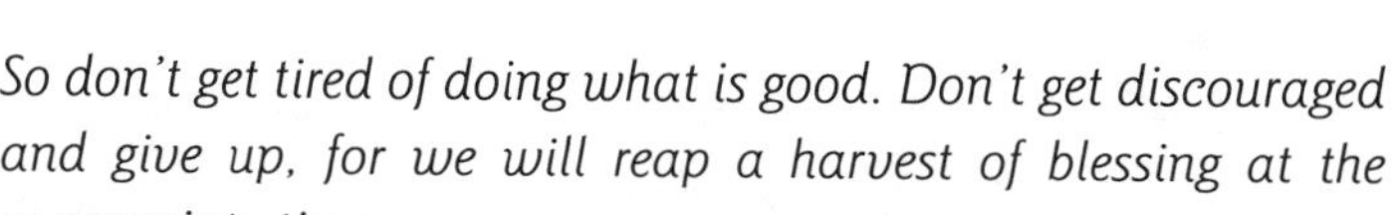

So don't get tired of doing what is good. Don't get discouraged and give up, for we will reap a harvest of blessing at the appropriate time.

Galatians 6:9 NLT

The Bible teaches us to treat other people with respect, kindness, courtesy, and love. When we do, we make other people happy, we make God happy, and we feel better about ourselves, too.

So if you're wondering how to make the world—and your world—a better place, here's a great place to start: let the Golden Rule be your rule. When you do, you'll like yourself a little better . . . and so will other people.

Sleep On It!

When you treat others with respect, you will feel better about yourself.

Bedtime Devotional 130

Today's Happiness

But happy are those . . . whose hope is in the LORD their God.

Psalm 146:5 NLT

If we could decide to be happy "once and for all," life would be so much simpler, but it doesn't seem to work that way. If we want happiness to last, we need to create good thoughts every day that we live. Yesterday's good thoughts don't count . . . we've got to think more good thoughts now.

Each new day is a gift from God, so treat it that way. Think about it like this: today is another wonderful chance to celebrate God's gifts.

So celebrate—starting now—and keep celebrating forever!

Sleep On It!

Better self-control can help make you happy: the better you behave, the more fun you'll have. And don't let anybody try to tell you otherwise.

Bedtime Devotional 131

An Honest Heart

In every way be an example of doing good deeds. When you teach, do it with honesty and seriousness.

Titus 2:7 NCV

Where does honesty begin? In your own heart and your own head. If you really want to be an honest person, then you must ask God to help you find the courage to be honest all of the time.

Honesty is not a "sometimes" thing. If you intend to be a truthful person, you must make truthfulness a habit that becomes so much a part of you that you don't have to decide whether or not you're going to tell the truth. Instead, you will simply tell the truth because that's who you are.

Lying is an easy habit to fall into, and a terrible one. So make up your mind that you're going to be an honest person, and then stick to your decision. That's what your parents want you to do, and that's what God wants, too. And since they love you more than you know, trust them. And always tell the truth.

Sleep On It!

God doesn't expect you to be perfect, but he does insist on complete honesty.

Rick Warren

Bedtime Devotional 132

God's Friendship

Greater love has no one than this, that he lay down his life for his friends.

John 15:13 NIV

There's an old song that says, "What a friend we have in Jesus." Those words are certainly true! When you invite Him into your heart, Jesus will be your friend tonight, tomorrow, and forever.

Jesus wants you to have a happy, healthy life. He wants you to behave yourself, and He wants you to take care of yourself. And now, it's up to you to do your best to live up to the hopes and dreams of your very best friend: Jesus.

Sleep On It!

Of course you know that Jesus loves you. But it's up to you to make sure that your friends know it, too. So remind them often.

Bedtime Devotional 133

Loving People Who Are Hard to Love

You have heard it said, "Love your neighbor and hate your enemy." But I tell you: Love your enemies and pray for those who persecute you, that you may be sons of your Father in heaven.

Matthew 5:43-45 NIV

Sometimes people can be rude . . . very rude. As long as you live here on earth, you will face countless opportunities to lose your temper when other folks behave badly. But God has a better plan: He wants you to forgive people and move on. Remember that God has already forgiven you, so it's only right that you should be willing to forgive others.

So here's some good advice: Forgive everybody as quickly as you can, and leave the rest up to God.

Sleep On It!

You can be sure you are abiding in Christ if you are able to have a Christlike love toward the people that irritate you the most.

Vonette Bright

Bedtime Devotional 134

Tonight, Try to Memorize This Verse

A gentle answer turns away wrath,
but a harsh word stirs up anger.

Proverbs 15:1 NIV

This is an important Bible verse. Practice saying it several times. And then, talk to your mom or dad about exactly what the verse means . . .

A Tip for Parents

Tonight, talk to your child about . . .
the words he speaks.

Bedtime Devotional 135

Your Picture

For God so loved the world that he gave his only Son, so that everyone who believes in him will not perish but have eternal life.

John 3:16 NLT

If God had a refrigerator in heaven, your picture would be on it! And that fact should make you feel very good about the person you are and the person you can become.

God's love for you is bigger and more wonderful than you can imagine, So do this, and do it right now: accept God's love with open arms and welcome His Son Jesus into your heart. When you do, you'll feel better about yourself . . . and your life will be changed forever.

Sleep On It!

Remember: God's love for you is too big to understand with your brain . . . but it's not too big to feel with your heart.

Bedtime Devotional 136

He Is Everywhere

God did this so that men would seek him and perhaps reach out for him and find him, though he is not far from each one of us.

Acts 17:27 NIV

God is everywhere you have ever been. And He is everywhere you will ever go. That's why you can speak to God any time you need to.

If you are afraid or discouraged, you can turn to God for strength. If you are worried, you can trust God's promises. And if you are happy, you can thank Him for His gifts.

God is right here, and so are you. And He's waiting patiently to hear from you, so why not have a word with Him right now?

Sleep On It!

God is in the midst of whatever has happened, is happening, and will happen.

Charles Swindoll

The Good in Others, and You

Dear friend, do not imitate what is evil, but what is good. The one who does good is of God; the one who does evil has not seen God.

3 John 1:11 Holman CSB

If you look for the good in other people, you'll probably find it. And, if you look for the good things in life, you'll probably find them, too.

When you start looking for good things, you'll find them everywhere: in church, at school, in your neighborhood, and at home.

So don't waste your time on things that make you feel angry, discouraged, worried, guilty, or afraid. Look, instead, for the good things in life, the things that God wants you to pay attention to. You'll be glad you did . . . and God will be glad, too.

Sleep On It!

Do all the good you can. By all the means you can. In all the ways you can. In all the places you can. At all the times you can. To all the people you can. As long as ever you can.

John Wesley

Bedtime Devotional 138

Each Day Is a Gift

How happy are those who can live in your house, always singing your praises. How happy are those who are strong in the Lord . . . .

Psalm 84:4-5 NLT

God wants you to have a happy, joyful life. But that doesn't mean that you'll be happy all the time. Sometimes, you won't feel like feeling happy, and when you don't, your attitude won't be very good.

When you're feeling a little tired or sad, here's something to remember: This day is a gift from God. And it's up to you to enjoy this day by trying to be cheerful, helpful, courteous, and well behaved. How can you do these things? A good place to start is by doing your best to think good thoughts.

Sleep On It!

To make happiness last, we must obey God while celebrating His blessings. To make happiness disappear, we need only disobey God while ignoring His blessings.

Bedtime Devotional 139

A Royal Law

This royal law is found in the Scriptures: "Love your neighbor as yourself." If you obey this law, then you are doing right.

James 2:8 ICB

James was the brother of Jesus and a leader of the early Christian church. In a letter that is now a part of the New Testament, James reminded his friends of a "royal law." That law is the Golden Rule.

When we treat others in the same way that we wish to be treated, we are doing the right thing. James knew it and so, of course did his brother Jesus. Now we should learn the same lesson: it's nice to be nice; it's good to be good; and it's great to be kind.

Sleep On It!

Encouraging others means helping people, looking for the best in them, and trying to bring out their positive qualities.

John Maxwell

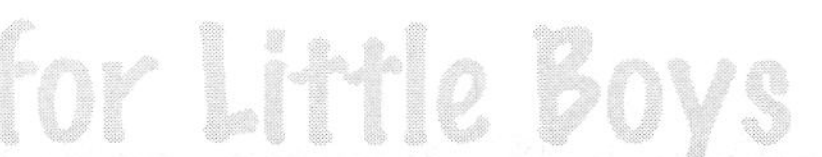

Bedtime Devotional 140

His Joy, Our Joy

I've told you these things for a purpose: that my joy might be your joy, and your joy wholly mature.

John 15:11 MSG

Christ made it clear to His followers: He intended that His joy would become their joy. And it's still true today: Christ intends that His believers share His love with His joy in their hearts. Yet sometimes, amid the inevitable hustle and bustle of life-here-on-earth, we can lose—at least for a while—the joy of Christ as we wrestle with the challenges of daily living.

C. H. Spurgeon, the 19th-century English clergyman, advised, "The Lord is glad to open the gate to every knocking soul. It opens very freely. Have faith and enter at this moment through holy courage. If you knock with a heavy heart, you shall yet sing with joy of spirit. Never be discouraged!" How true!

Sleep On It!

Joy does not depend upon your circumstances, but on your relationship with God.

It's a Good Feeling to Obey and Forgive

This is love for God: to obey his commands.

I John 5:3 NIV

We know that it's right to forgive other people and wrong to stay angry with them. But sometimes, it's so much easier to do the wrong thing than it is to do the right thing, especially when we're tired or frustrated.

When you do the right thing by forgiving other people, you'll feel good because you'll know that you're obeying God. And that's a very good feeling indeed. So make this promise to yourself and keep it: play by the rules—God's rules. You'll always be glad you did.

Sleep On It!

Your obedience to God is a way to show Him that you're thankful for the blessings He has given you.

Bedtime Devotional 142

Tonight, Here Are Some Big Ideas About Not Giving Up

Here are two important ideas. Take a few minutes to talk to your mom or dad about what these quotations mean.

By perseverance the snail reached the ark.
C. H. Spurgeon

Battles are won in the trenches,
in the grit and grime of courageous determination;
they are won day by day in the arena of life.
Charles Swindoll

Lost in the Crowd?

We must obey God rather than men.

Acts 5:29 Holman CSB

Rick Warren observed, "Those who follow the crowd usually get lost in it." We know those words to be true, but oftentimes we fail to live by them. Instead of trusting God for guidance, we imitate our friends and suffer the consequences.

Instead of getting lost in the crowd, you should find guidance from your parents and from God. When you do, you'll be happier . . . much happier!

Sleep On It!

Being obedient to God means that you cannot always please other people.

Bedtime Devotional 144

Be Patient

Don't work hard only when your master is watching and then shirk when he isn't looking; work hard and with gladness all the time, as though working for Christ, doing the will of God with all your hearts.

Ephesians 6:6-7 TLB

If you've lost patience with someone, or if you're angry, take a deep breath and then ask yourself a simple question: "How would Jesus behave if He were here?" The answer to that question will tell you what to do.

Jesus was quick to speak kind words, and He was quick to forgive others. We must do our best to be like Him. When we do, we will be patient, loving, understanding, and kind.

Sleep On It!

We have in Jesus Christ a perfect example of how to put God's truth into practice.

Bill Bright

It Pays to Praise

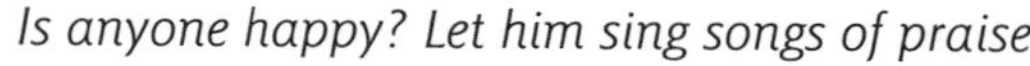

Is anyone happy? Let him sing songs of praise.

James 5:13 NIV

The Bible makes it clear: it pays to say "thank You" to God. But sometimes, we may not feel like thanking anybody, not even our Father in heaven.

If we ever stop praising God, it's a big mistake . . . a VERY BIG mistake.

When you stop to think about it, God has been very generous with you . . . and He deserves a great big "thanks" for all those amazing gifts.

Do you want an attitude that pleases God? Then make sure that your attitude praises God. And don't just praise Him on Sunday morning. Praise Him every day, starting with this one.

Sleep On It!

When you pray, don't just ask God for things; also praise Him.

Bedtime Devotional 146

Tonight, Try to Memorize This Verse

And without faith it is impossible to please God, because anyone who comes to him must believe that he exists and that he rewards those who earnestly seek him.

Hebrews 11:6 NIV

This is an important Bible verse. Practice saying it several times. And then, talk to your mom or dad about exactly what the verse means . . .

A Tip for Parents

Tonight, talk to your child about . . .
the importance of faith.

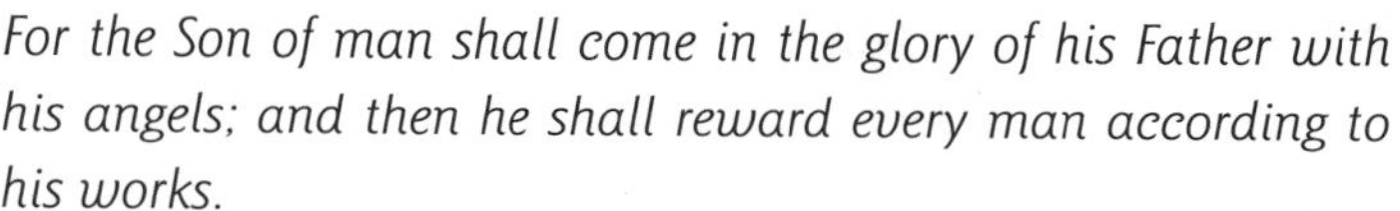

Keep Learning About Self-Control

For the Son of man shall come in the glory of his Father with his angels; and then he shall reward every man according to his works.

Matthew 16:27 KJV

Who needs to learn more about self-control? You do! Why? Well, for one thing, you'll discover that good things happen to boys (like you) who are wise enough to think ahead and smart enough to look before they leap.

Whether you're at home or at school, you'll learn that the best rewards go to the kids who control their behavior—not to the people who let their behaviors control them!

Sleep On It!

The problem is that we want the rewards of success without paying the price.

John Maxwell

Bedtime Devotional 148

Look Ahead

Learn the truth and never reject it. Get wisdom, self-control, and understanding.

Proverbs 23:23 NCV

Maybe you've heard this old saying: "Look before you leap." What does that saying mean? It means that you should stop and think before you do something. Otherwise, you might be sorry you did it.

Your parents are trying to teach you how to slow down and make better decisions. Why? Because your parents want what's best for you, that's why!

So here's something that you can do: think about the consequences of your behaviors before you do something silly . . . or dangerous . . . or both.

Sleep On It!

When you learn how to control yourself, you'll be happier . . . and your parents will be happier, too.

Bedtime Devotional 149

Start Sharing Now

Never walk away from someone who deserves help; your hand is God's hand for that person.

Proverbs 3:27 MSG

When is the best time to share? Whenever you can—and that means right now, if possible. When you start thinking about the things you can share, you probably think mostly about things that belong to you (like toys or clothes), but there are many more things you can share (like love, kindness, encouragement, and prayers). That means you have the opportunity to share something with somebody almost any time you want. And that's exactly what God wants you to do—so start sharing now and don't ever stop.

Sleep On It!

It is the duty of every Christian to be Christ to his neighbor.

Martin Luther

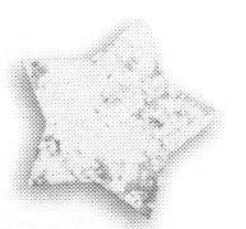

Bedtime Devotional 150

Tonight, Here Are Some Big Ideas About Perfectionism

Here are two important ideas. Take a few minutes to talk to your mom or dad about what these quotations mean.

> What makes a Christian a Christian
> is not perfection but forgiveness.
>
> Max Lucado

> The happiest people in the world are not those
> who have no problems, but the people who have learned
> to live with those things that are less than perfect.
>
> James Dobson

Bedtime Devotional 151

Your Family Has Rules

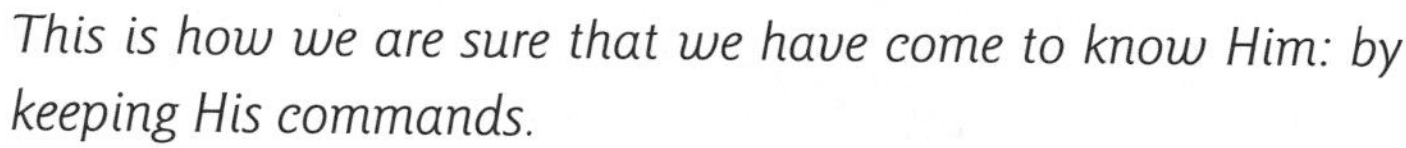
This is how we are sure that we have come to know Him: by keeping His commands.

I John 2:3 Holman CSB

Face facts: your family has rules . . . rules that you're not supposed to break.

If you're old enough to know right from wrong, then you're old enough to do something about it. In other words, you should always try to obey your family's rules.

How can you tell "the right thing" from "the wrong thing"? By listening carefully to your parents, that's how.

The more self-control you have, the easier it is to obey your parents. Why? Because, when you learn to think first and do things next, you avoid making silly mistakes. So here's what you should do: First, slow down long enough to listen to your parents. Then, do the things that you know your parents want you to do.

Face facts: your family has rules . . . and it's better for everybody when you obey them.

Sleep On It!

Since you love your family, show it by behaving yourself and obeying your family's rules!

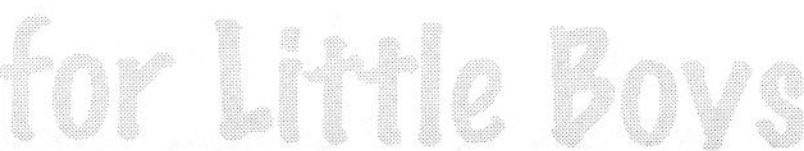

Listening Quietly and Carefully

A wise man will hear and increase in learning, and a man of understanding will acquire wise counsel.

Proverbs 1:5 NASB

Have you learned how to sit quietly and listen to your parents and your teachers? Have you learned how to listen respectfully—with your ears open wide and your mouth closed tight? If so, give yourself a big pat on the back (or if you can't reach way back there, ask your mom or dad to do it for you!).

An important part of learning self-control is learning how to be quiet when you're supposed to be quiet. It isn't always easy, but the sooner you learn how to sit quietly and behave respectfully, the better. So you might as well start today.

Sleep On It!

For kids of all ages, the temptation to talk is great; it takes conscious effort to hold one's tongue until one's ears are fully engaged. When a person is able to do so, his or her efforts are usually rewarded.

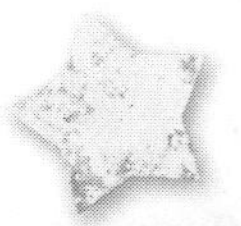

Bedtime Devotional 153

How Much Is Too Much?

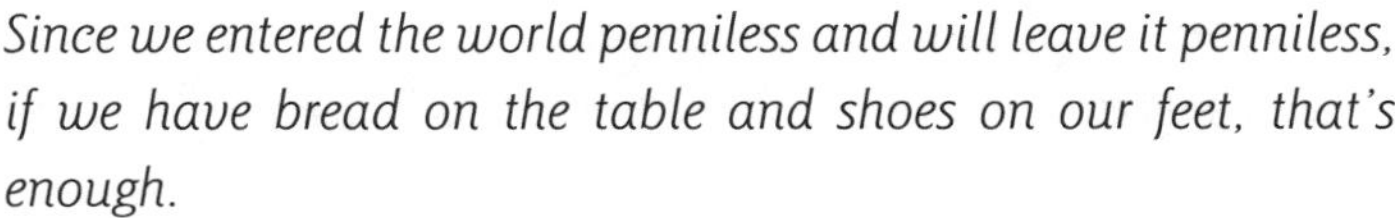

Since we entered the world penniless and will leave it penniless, if we have bread on the table and shoes on our feet, that's enough.

I Timothy 6:7-8 MSG

How much stuff is too much stuff? Well, if your desire for stuff is getting in the way of your desire to know God, then you've got too much stuff—it's as simple as that.

If you find yourself worrying too much about stuff, it's time to change the way you think about the things you own. Stuff isn't really very important to God, and it shouldn't be too important to you.

Sleep On It!

The world wants you to believe that "money and stuff" can buy happiness. Don't believe it! Genuine happiness comes not from money, but from the things that money can't buy—starting, of course, with your relationship to God and His only begotten Son.

Bedtime Devotional 154

Obedience Is a Choice

Those who obey his commands live in him, and he in them. And this is how we know that he lives in us: We know it by the Spirit he gave us.

I John 3:24 NIV

You have a choice to make: are you going to be an obedient boy or not? And remember: the decision to be obedient—or the decision not to be obedient—is a decision that you must make for yourself.

If you decide to behave yourself you've made a smart choice. If you decide to obey your parents and pay attention to your teachers, you've made a wise choice. BUT . . . if you decide not to be obedient, you've made a silly choice.

What kind of person will you choose to be? An obedient, well-behaved person . . . or the opposite? Before you answer that question, here's something to think about: obedience pays . . . and disobedience doesn't.

Sleep On It!

Obedience leads to spiritual growth: Anne Graham Lotz correctly observed, "If you want to discover your spiritual gifts, start obeying God. As you serve Him, you will find that He has given you the gifts that are necessary to follow through in obedience."

Bedtime Devotional 155

You're Not Expected to Be Perfect

If we confess our sins to him, he is faithful and just to forgive us and to cleanse us from every wrong.

I John 1:9 NLT

When you make a mistake, do you get really mad at yourself . . . or maybe really, really, really mad? Hopefully not! After all, everybody makes mistakes, and nobody is expected to be perfect.

Even when you make mistakes, God loves you . . . so you should love yourself, too.

So the next time you make a mistake, learn from it. And after you've learned your lesson, try never to make that same mistake again. But don't be too hard on yourself. God doesn't expect you to be perfect, and since He loves you anyway, you should feel that way, too.

Sleep On It!

A mistake is never permanent (unless you do nothing to fix it).

Bedtime Devotional 156

The Stuff You Own Isn't as Important as You May Think

Don't be obsessed with getting more material things. Be relaxed with what you have.

Hebrews 13:5 MSG

Here's something to remember about stuff: It's not that important!

Lots of people are in love with money and the things that money can buy. God is not. God cares about people, not possessions, and so must you.

You should not be too concerned about the clothes you wear, or the things you own. And above all, don't ever let your self-esteem depend upon the things that you (or your parents) own.

The stuff that you own isn't nearly as important as the love that you feel in your heart—love for your family, love for your friends, and love for your Father in heaven.

Sleep On It!

Your possessions are actually God's possessions, so try to use them for His purposes.

Bedtime Devotional 157

God Is Watching

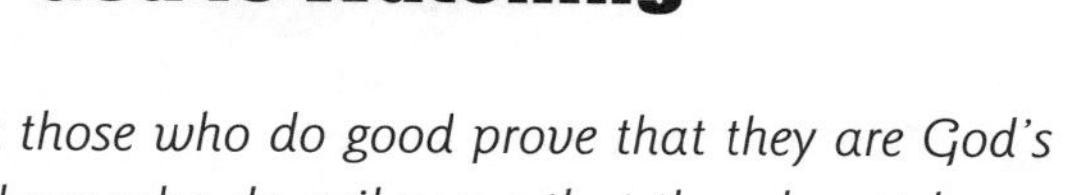

Remember that those who do good prove that they are God's children, and those who do evil prove that they do not know God.

3 John 1:11 NLT

Even when nobody's watching, God is. And He knows whether you've done the right thing or the wrong thing. So if you're tempted to misbehave when nobody is looking, remember this: There is never a time when "nobody's watching." Somebody is always watching over you—and that Somebody, of course, is your Father in heaven. Don't let Him down!

Sleep On It!

When it comes to telling the world about your relationship with God, your actions speak much more loudly than your words . . . so behave accordingly.

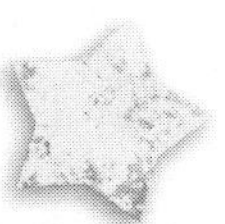

The Right Choice

But Daniel purposed in his heart that he would not defile himself . . . .

Daniel 1:8 KJV

Your life is a series of choices. From the instant you wake up in the morning until the moment you nod off to sleep at night, you make lots of decisions: decisions about the things you do, decisions about the words you speak, and decisions about the thoughts you choose to think.

So, if you want to lead a life that is pleasing to God, you must make choices that are pleasing to Him. He deserves no less . . . and neither, for that matter, do you.

Sleep On It!

When you make wise choices, you make everybody happy. You make your parents happy, you make your teachers happy, you make your friends happy, and you make God happy!

Bedtime Devotional 159

Tonight, Try to Memorize This Verse

I have learned to be content
in whatever circumstances I am.

Philippians 4:11 Holman CSB

This is an important Bible verse. Practice saying it several times. And then, talk to your mom or dad about exactly what the verse means . . .

A Tip for Parents

Tonight, talk to your child about . . .
finding true contentment.

Bedtime Devotional 160

Get Over It

Do not remember the past events, pay no attention to things of old. Look, I am about to do something new; even now it is coming. Do you not see it? Indeed, I will make a way in the wilderness, rivers in the desert.

Isaiah 43:18-19 Holman CSB

An important part of learning how to forgive is learning how to get over the things that happened yesterday. What happened yesterday is past. And, if what happened yesterday has made you unhappy, today is as good a day as any to start getting over your hurt feelings.

Are you still angry with someone? Has that person said he was sorry and tried to make things better? If so, talk to your parents about it! They'll help you understand that you can't change the past, but you can get over it.

Sleep On It!

The past is past, so don't live there; don't worry too much about yesterday. Instead, spend your time figuring out how to make tomorrow better.

Jesus Offers Peace

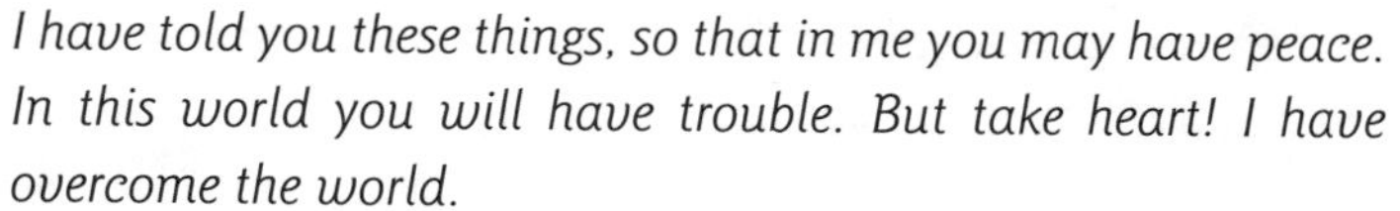

I have told you these things, so that in me you may have peace. In this world you will have trouble. But take heart! I have overcome the world.

John 16:33 NIV

Jesus offers us peace . . . peace in our hearts and peace in our homes. But He doesn't force us to enjoy His peace—we can either accept His peace or not.

When we accept the peace of Jesus Christ by opening up our hearts to Him, we feel much better about ourselves, our families, and our lives.

Would you like to feel a little better about yourself and a little better about your corner of the world? Then open up your heart to Jesus, because that's where real peace begins.

Sleep On It!

You have a big role to play in helping to maintain a peaceful home. It's a big job, so don't be afraid to ask for help . . . especially God's help.

Bedtime Devotional 162

Nobody's Perfect

For everything created by God is good, and nothing should be rejected if it is received with thanksgiving.

I Timothy 4:4 Holman CSB

Face facts: nobody's perfect . . . not even you! And remember this: it's perfectly okay not to be perfect. In fact, God doesn't expect you to be perfect, and you shouldn't expect yourself to be perfect, either.

Are you one of those people who can't stand to make a mistake? Do you think that you must please everybody all the time? When you make a mess of things, do you become terribly upset? If so, here's some advice: DON'T BE SO HARD ON YOURSELF! Mistakes happen . . . and besides, if you learn something from your mistakes, you'll become a better person.

Sleep On It!

The world isn't perfect; your family and friends aren't perfect; and you aren't perfect—and that's okay: We'll all have plenty of time to be perfect in heaven. Until then, we should all be compassionate, forgiving Christians.

Bedtime Devotional 163

What's Really Important

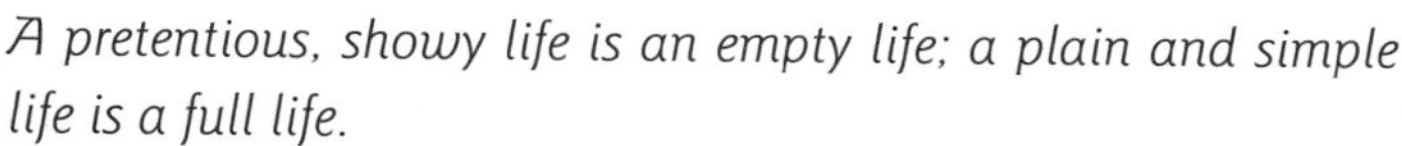

A pretentious, showy life is an empty life; a plain and simple life is a full life.

Proverbs 13:7 MSG

"So much stuff to shop for, and so little time . . ." These words describe lots of people, but please don't let those words describe you!

The Bible teaches this important lesson: it's not good to be too concerned about money or the stuff that money can buy. So don't worry too much about the things you can buy in stores. Worry more about obeying your parents and obeying your Heavenly Father—that's what's really important.

Sleep On It!

The world says, "Buy more stuff." God says, "Stuff isn't important." Believe God.

Bedtime Devotional 164

Tonight, Try to Memorize This Verse

If we confess our sins,
He is faithful and righteous
to forgive us our sins and to cleanse us
from all unrighteousness.

I John 1:9 Holman CSB

This is an important Bible verse. Practice saying it several times. And then, talk to your mom or dad about exactly what the verse means . . .

A Tip for Parents

Tonight, talk to your child about . . .
the need to confess sin.

Bedtime Devotional 165

Be Responsible

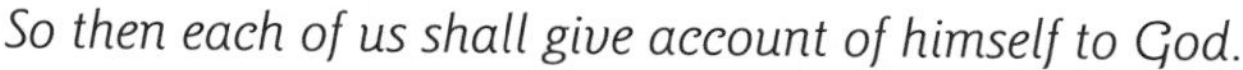

So then each of us shall give account of himself to God.

Romans 14:12 NKJV

Nobody can be patient for you. You've got to be patient for yourself. Certainly your parents can teach you about patience, but when it comes to controlling your temper, nobody can control it for you; you've got to control it yourself.

In the Book of Galatians, Paul writes, "We must not tire of doing good." And that's an important lesson: even when we're tired or frustrated, we must do our best to do the right thing.

So the next time you're tempted to lose your temper, stop for a moment and remember that when it comes to good deeds and good behavior, it's all up to you.

Sleep On It!

Although God causes all things to work together for good for His children, He still holds us accountable for our behavior.

Kay Arthur

Bedtime Devotional 166

You're So Very Special

Blessed is the man who does not condemn himself.

Romans 14:22 Holman CSB

When God made you, He made you in a very special way. In fact, you're a wonderful, one-of-a-kind creation, a special person unlike any other.

Do you realize how special you are? Do you know that God loves you because of who you are (not because of the things you've done)? And do you know that God has important things for you to do? Well whether you realize it or not, all these things are true.

So the next time you feel bad about something you've done, take a look in the mirror, and remember that you're looking at a wonderfully special person . . . you!

God loves you; your parents love you; your family loves you . . . and that's the way that you should feel about yourself, too.

Sleep On It!

God is working in you and through you to help you become the person He intends for you to be.

Bedtime Devotional 167

Do the Right Thing: Share!

It is well with the man who deals generously and lends.

Psalm 112:5 RSV

It's a fact: sharing makes you a better person. Why? Because when you share, you're doing several things: first, you're obeying God; and, you're making your corner of the world a better place; and you're learning exactly what it feels like to be a generous, loving person.

When you share, you have the fun of knowing that your good deeds are making other people happy. When you share, you're learning how to become a better person. When you share, you're making things better for other people and for yourself. So do the right thing: share!

Sleep On It!

Find out how much God has given you and from it take what you need; the remainder is needed by others.

St. Augustine

Bedtime Devotional 168

Keep Growing Up

Therefore, leaving the elementary message about the Messiah, let us go on to maturity.

Hebrews 6:1 Holman CSB

When will you be completely grown up? Hopefully never! God has a way of helping you continue to grow as a Christian throughout your entire life if you continue to worship Him.

If you learn about God's Word and talk to Him through your prayers, He has much to teach you, so keep learning about your Heavenly Father. And never stop.

Sleep On It!

The strength of our spiritual lives will be in exact proportion to the place held by the Bible in our lives and in our thoughts.

George Mueller

Bedtime Devotional 169

Keeping a Thankful Attitude

And whatever you do, in word or in deed, do everything in the name of the Lord Jesus, giving thanks to God the Father through Him.

Colossians 3:17 Holman CSB

Do you have a thankful attitude? Hopefully so! After all, you've got plenty of things to be thankful for. Even during those times when you're angry or tired, you're a very lucky person.

Who has given you all the blessings you enjoy? Your parents are responsible, of course. But all of your blessings really start with God. That's why you should say "Thank You" to God many times each day. He's given you so much . . . so thank Him, starting now.

Sleep On It!

Want to cheer yourself up? Count your blessings. If you need a little cheering up, start counting your blessings . . . and keep counting until you feel better.

Waiting Your Turn

Don't be impatient for the Lord to act! Travel steadily along his path. He will honor you . . . .

Psalm 37:34 NLT

When we're standing in line or waiting our turn, it's tempting to scream, "Me first!" It's tempting, but it's the wrong thing to do! The Bible tells us that we shouldn't push ahead of other people; instead, we should do the right thing—and the polite thing—by saying, "You first!"

Sometimes, waiting your turn can be hard, especially if you're excited or in a hurry. But even then, waiting patiently is the right thing to do. Why? Because parents say so, teachers say so, and, most importantly, God says so!

Sleep On It!

It's not difficult to make an impact on your world. All you really have to do is put the needs of others ahead of your own. You can make a difference with a little time and a big heart.

James Dobson

Truth Matters

He has showed you, O man, what is good. And what does the LORD require of you? To act justly and to love mercy and to walk humbly with your God.

Micah 6:8 NIV

If you're tempted to say something that isn't true, stop and ask yourself a simple question: "How would Jesus behave if He were here?" The answer to that question will tell you what to say.

Jesus told His followers that the truth would make them free. As believers, we must do our best to know the truth and to tell it. When we do, we behave as our Savior behaved, and that's exactly how God wants us to behave.

Sleep On It!

When in doubt, do the thing that you think Jesus would do. And, of course, don't do something if you think that He wouldn't do it.

Bedtime Devotional 172

Count Your Blessings

Enter his gates with thanksgiving; go into his courts with praise. Give thanks to him and bless his name. For the Lord is good. His unfailing love continues forever, and his faithfulness continues to each generation.

Psalm 100:4-5 NLT

If you sat down and began counting your blessings, how long would it take? A very, very long time! Your blessings include your life, your family, your friends, your talents, and possessions, for starters. But, your greatest blessing—a gift that is yours for the asking—is God's gift of eternal life through Christ Jesus.

You can never count up every single blessing that God has given you, but it doesn't hurt to try . . . so get ready, get set, go—start counting your blessings RIGHT NOW!

Sleep On It!

There is value in thanking God for His perfect plan even when you don't understand that plan.

Stop and Think

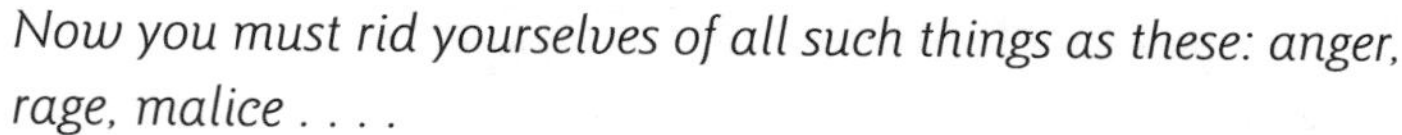

Now you must rid yourselves of all such things as these: anger, rage, malice . . . .

Colossians 3:8 NIV

When we lose control of our emotions, we do things that we shouldn't do. Sometimes, we throw tantrums. How silly! Other times we pout or whine. Too bad!

The Bible tells us that it is foolish to become angry and that it is wise to remain calm. That's why we should learn to slow down and think about things before we do them.

Do you want to make life better for yourself and for your family? Then be patient and think things through. Stop and think before you do things, not after. It's the wise thing to do.

Sleep On It!

If you're a little angry, think carefully before you speak. If you're very angry, think very carefully. Otherwise, you might say something in anger that you regret later.

God Wrote a Book

For I am not ashamed of the gospel, because it is God's power for salvation to everyone who believes.

Romans 1:16 Holman CSB

If you want to know God, you should read the book He wrote. It's called the Bible (of course!), and God uses it to teach you and guide you. The Bible is not like any other book. It is an amazing gift from your Heavenly Father.

D. L. Moody observed, "The Bible was not given to increase our knowledge but to change our lives." God's Holy Word is, indeed, a life-changing, one-of-a-kind treasure. Handle it with care, but more importantly, handle it every day!

Sleep On It!

Start learning about Jesus, and keep learning about Him as long as you live. His story never grows old, and His teachings never fail.

Tonight, Try to Memorize This Verse

God loves a cheerful giver.

2 Corinthians 9:7 Holman CSB

This is an important Bible verse. Practice saying it several times. And then, talk to your mom or dad about exactly what the verse means . . .

A Tip for Parents

Tonight, talk to your child about . . .
the joy of giving.

Bedtime Devotional 176

Self-Control and Patience

All athletes practice strict self-control. They do it to win a prize that will fade away, but we do it for an eternal prize.

I Corinthians 9:25 NLT

The Book of Proverbs tells us that self-control and patience are very good things to have. But for most of us, self-control and patience can also be very hard things to learn.

Are you having trouble being patient? And are you having trouble slowing down long enough to think before you act? If so, remember that self-control takes practice, and lots of it, so keep trying. And if you make a mistake, don't be too upset. After all, if you're going to be a really patient person, you shouldn't just be patient with others; you should also be patient with yourself.

Sleep On It!

Your thoughts are the determining factor as to whose mold you are conformed to. Control your thoughts and you control the direction of your life.

Charles Stanley

When You Don't Know What to Say

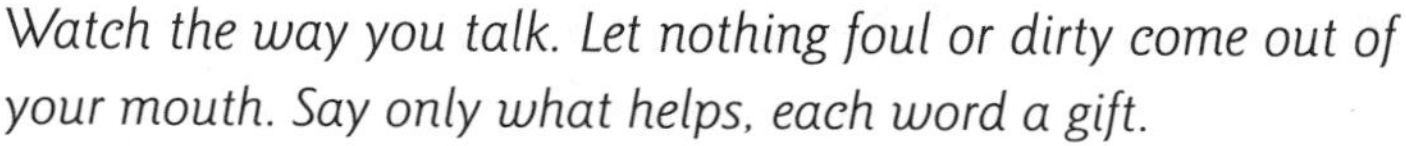

Watch the way you talk. Let nothing foul or dirty come out of your mouth. Say only what helps, each word a gift.

Ephesians 4:29 MSG

Sometimes, it's hard to know exactly what to say. And sometimes, it can be very tempting to say something that isn't true—or something that isn't nice. But when you say things you shouldn't say, you'll regret it later.

So make this promise to yourself, and keep it—promise to think about the things you say before you say them. And whatever you do, always tell the truth. When you do these things, you'll be doing yourself a big favor, and you'll be obeying the Word of God.

Sleep On It!

Think first, speak second. If you want to keep from hurting other people's feelings, don't open your mouth until you've turned on your brain.

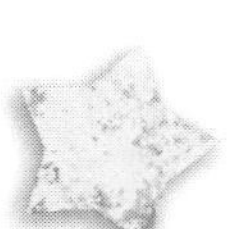

Bedtime Devotional 178

Letting Other People Know What It Means to Be a Christian

But respect Christ as the holy Lord in your hearts. Always be ready to answer everyone who asks you to explain about the hope you have.

1 Peter 3:15 NCV

Every Christian, each in his or her own way, has a responsibility to share the Good News of our Jesus. And it's important to remember that we bear testimony through both words and actions. Wise Christians follow the advice of St. Francis of Assisi who advised, "Preach the gospel at all times and, if necessary, use words."

As you think about how your example influences others, remember that actions speak louder than words . . . much louder!

Sleep On It!

Remember this: You share your testimony through words and actions. And the actions speak louder.

Bedtime Devotional 179

The Truth

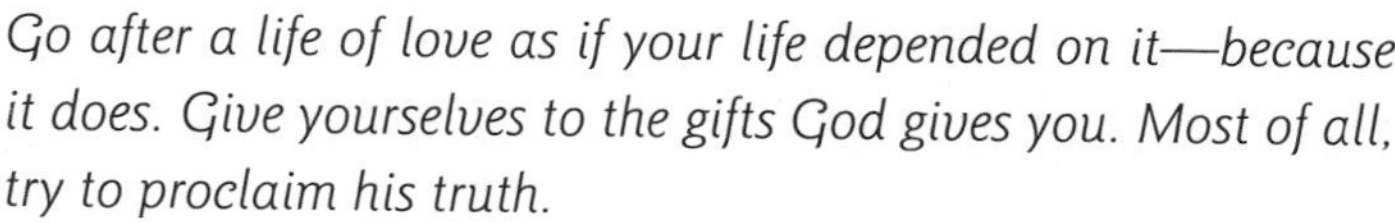

Go after a life of love as if your life depended on it—because it does. Give yourselves to the gifts God gives you. Most of all, try to proclaim his truth.

1 Corinthians 14:1 MSG

Jesus had a message for His followers. He said, "The truth will set you free." When we do the right thing and tell the truth, we don't need to worry about our lies catching up with us. When we behave honestly, we don't have to worry about feeling guilty or ashamed. But, if we fail to do what we know is right, bad things start to happen, and we feel guilty.

Jesus understood that the truth is a very good thing indeed. We should understand it, too. And we should keep telling it as long as we live.

Sleep On It!

Warren Wiersbe writes, "Learning God's truth and getting it into our heads is one thing, but living God's truth and getting it into our characters is quite something else." So don't be satisfied to sit on the sidelines and observe the truth at a distance—live it.

Bedtime Devotional 180

When We're Worried

Give all your worries and cares to God, for he cares about what happens to you.

I Peter 5:6 NLT

When we're worried, there are two places we should take our concerns: to the people who love and care for us and to God.

When troubles arise, it helps to talk about them with parents, grandparents, and concerned adults. But we shouldn't stop there: we should also talk to God through our prayers.

If you're worried about something, you can pray about it any time you want. And remember that God is always listening, and He always wants to hear from you.

So when you're worried, try this plan: talk and pray. Talk to the grownups who love you, and pray to the Heavenly Father who made you. The more you talk and the more you pray, the better you'll feel.

Sleep On It!

Troubles will pass more quickly if you spend more time solving problems and less time fretting over them.

Don't Whine!

Words kill, words give life; they're either poison or fruit—you choose.

Proverbs 18:21 MSG

Do you like to listen to other children whine? No way! And since you don't like to hear other kids whining, then you certainly shouldn't whine, either.

Sometimes, kids think that whining is a good way to get the things they want . . . but it's not! So if your parents or your teacher ask you to do something, don't complain about it. And if there's something you want, don't whine and complain until you get it.

Remember: whining won't make you happy . . . and it won't make anybody else happy, either.

Sleep On It!

Whining can be contagious, so make sure that your home is, to the greatest extent possible, a whine-free zone. How can you do this? A good way to start is by counting your blessings, not your problems.

Because You're a Christian

Make the Master proud of you by being good citizens. Respect the authorities, whatever their level; they are God's emissaries for keeping order.

I Peter 2:13-14 MSG

Do you behave differently because you're a Christian? Or do you behave in pretty much the same way that you would if you had never heard of Jesus? Hopefully, your behavior is better because of the things you've learned from the Bible.

Doing the right thing is not always easy, especially when you're tired or frustrated. But, doing the wrong thing almost always leads to trouble. So here's some advice: remember the lessons you learn from the Bible. And keep remembering them every day of your life.

Sleep On It!

If you're not sure that it's the right thing to do, don't do it! And if you're not sure that it's the truth, don't tell it.

Bedtime Devotional 183

Every Day Is a Special Day

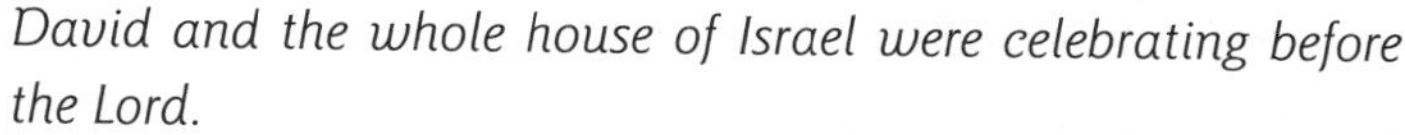

David and the whole house of Israel were celebrating before the Lord.

2 Samuel 6:5 Holman CSB

Every day should be a time for celebration, and hopefully, you feel like celebrating! After all, this day (like every other day) gives you the chance to thank God for all the wonderful things He has given you.

So don't wait for birthdays or holidays—make every day a special day, including this one. Take time to pause and thank God for His gifts. He deserves your thanks, and you deserve to celebrate!

Sleep On It!

Live in the present and make the most of your opportunities to enjoy your family and friends.

Barbara Johnson

Bedtime Devotional 184

That Little Voice

For God is pleased with you when, for the sake of your conscience, you patiently endure unfair treatment.

1 Peter 2:19 NLT

When you know that you're doing what's right, you'll feel better about yourself. Why? Because you have a little voice in your head called your "conscience." Your conscience is a feeling that tells you whether something is right or wrong—and it's a feeling that makes you feel better about yourself when you know you've done the right thing.

Your conscience is an important tool. Pay attention to it! The more you listen to your conscience, the easier it is to behave yourself. So here's great advice: first, slow down long enough to figure out the right thing to do—and then do it! When you do, you'll be proud of yourself . . . and other people will be proud of you, too.

Sleep On It!

That tiny little voice inside your head . . . is called your conscience. Treat it like a trusted friend: Listen to the things it says; it's usually right!

Bedtime Devotional 185

When Things Go Wrong

But as for you, be strong; don't be discouraged, for your work has a reward.

2 Chronicles 15:7 Holman CSB

Face facts: some days are more wonderful than other days. Sometimes, everything seems to go right, and on other days, many things seem to go wrong. But here's something to remember: even when you're disappointed with the way things turn out, God is near . . . and He loves you very much!

If you're disappointed, worried, sad, or afraid, you can talk to your parents and to God. And you certainly feel better when you do!

Sleep On It!

Often God has to shut a door in our face so that He can subsequently open the door through which He wants us to go.

Catherine Marshall

Bedtime Devotional 186

A Cheerful Heart

Jacob said, "For what a relief it is to see your friendly smile. It is like seeing the smile of God!"

Genesis 33:10 NLT

The Bible tells us that a cheerful heart is like medicine: it makes us feel better. Where does cheerfulness begin? It begins inside each of us; it begins in the heart. So let's be thankful to God for His blessings, and let's show our thanks by sharing good cheer wherever we go.

Today, make sure that you share a smile and a kind word with as many people as you can. This old world needs all the cheering up it can get . . . and so do your friends.

Sleep On It!

If you need a little cheering up, find somebody else who needs cheering up, too. Then, do your best to brighten that person's day. When you do, you'll discover that cheering up other people is a wonderful way to cheer yourself up, too!

Bedtime Devotional 187

Tonight, Try to Memorize This Verse

I can do all things through Christ which strengtheneth me.

Philippians 4:13 KJV

This is an important Bible verse. Practice saying it several times. And then, talk to your mom or dad about exactly what the verse means . . .

A Tip for Parents

Tonight, talk to your child about . . .
the strength Christ gives.

Encourage Each Other

So encourage each other and give each other strength, just as you are doing now.

1 Thessalonians 5:11 NCV

When other people are sad, what can we do? We can do our best to cheer them up by showing kindness and love.

The Bible tells us that we must care for each other, and when everybody is happy, that's an easy thing to do. But, when people are sad, for whatever reason, it's up to us to speak a kind word or to offer a helping hand.

Do you know someone who is discouraged or sad? If so, perhaps it's time to take matters into your own hands. Think of something you can do to cheer that person up . . . and then do it! You'll make two people happy.

Sleep On It!

You can't lift other people up without lifting yourself up, too.

Bedtime Devotional 189

Getting to Know God

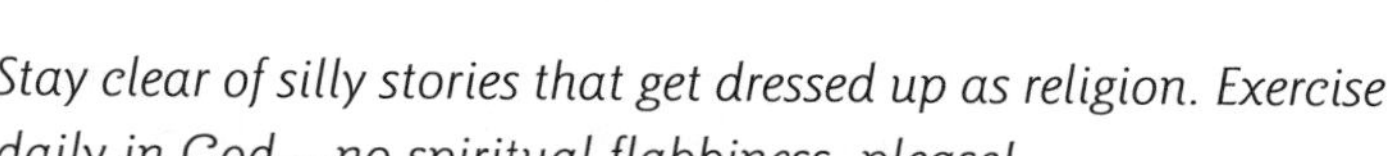

Stay clear of silly stories that get dressed up as religion. Exercise daily in God—no spiritual flabbiness, please!

I Timothy 4:7 MSG

Want to know God better? Then schedule a meeting with Him every day.

Each day has 1,440 minutes—will you spend a few of those minutes with your Heavenly Father? He deserves that much of your time and more. God wants you to pay attention to Him. So, if you haven't already done so, form the habit of spending quality time with your Creator. He deserves it . . . and so, for that matter, do you.

Sleep On It!

Do you have a special place where you and your parents read your daily devotionals? If not, you should ask your mom or dad to help you think of a good place where the two of you can read the Bible and talk to God.

Bedtime Devotional 190

Tell It Like It Is

I have no greater joy than this: to hear that my children are walking in the truth.

3 John 1:4 Holman CSB

Perhaps you've heard the story of the boy who cried "wolf!" In that story, the boy exaggerated his problems and eventually got himself into BIG trouble!

When we pretend that our troubles are worse than they really are, we may earn a little sympathy now, but we'll invite lots of trouble later.

If you're ever tempted to cry wolf, don't.

Exaggeration wasn't good for the boy who cried wolf, and it's not good for you.

Sleep On It!

Don't exaggerate! All of us have enough troubles without pretending that we have more.

Tonight, Try to Memorize This Verse

For all have sinned and fall short of the glory of God,

Romans 3:23 NIV

This is an important Bible verse. Practice saying it several times. And then, talk to your mom or dad about exactly what the verse means . . .

A Tip for Parents

Tonight, talk to your child about . . .
learning from mistakes.

Do Yourself a Favor

And whenever you stand praying, if you have anything against anyone, forgive him, so that your Father in heaven may also forgive you your wrongdoing.

Mark 11:25 Holman CSB

When you forgive somebody else, you're actually doing yourself a favor. Why? Because when you forgive the other person, you get rid of angry feelings that can make you unhappy.

Are you still angry about something that happened yesterday, or the day before that, or the day before that? Do yourself a big favor: forgive everybody (including yourself, if necessary). When you do, you won't change what happened yesterday, but you will make today a whole lot better.

Sleep On It!

If you're having trouble forgiving someone else . . . think how many times other people have forgiven you!

Bedtime Devotional 193

Love That Lasts

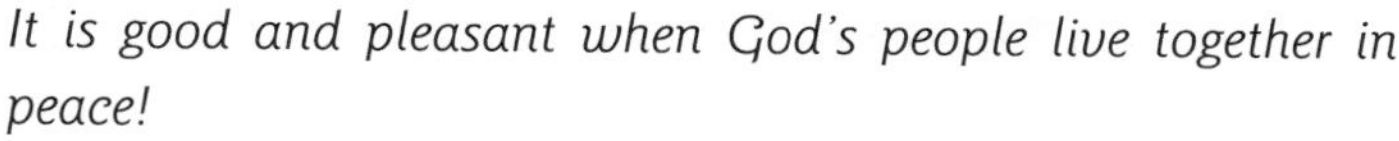

It is good and pleasant when God's people live together in peace!

Psalm 133:1 NCV

Are your friends kind to you? And are your friends nice to other people, too? If so, congratulations! If not, it's probably time to start looking for a few new friends. After all, it's really not very much fun to be around people who aren't nice to everybody.

The Bible teaches that a pure heart is a wonderful blessing. It's up to each of us to fill our hearts with love for God, love for Jesus, and love for all people. When we do, we feel better about ourselves.

Do you want to be the best person you can be? Then invite the love of Christ into your heart and share His love with your family and friends. And remember that lasting love always comes from a pure heart . . . like yours!

Sleep On It!

The best rule for making and keeping friends . . . is the Golden one.

Gentle Words

Always be humble, gentle, and patient, accepting each other in love.

Ephesians 4:2 NCV

The Bible tells us that gentle words are helpful and that cruel words are not. But sometimes, especially when we're upset, our words and our actions may not be so gentle. Sometimes, we may say things that are unkind or hurtful to others. But it's wrong to hurt others.

So the next time you're tempted to say something or do something in a fit of anger, don't. And while you're at it, remember that gentle words are better than angry words and good deeds are better than the other kind. Always!

Sleep On It!

I choose gentleness. Nothing is won by force. I choose to be gentle. If I raise my voice may it be only in praise. If I clench my fist, may it be only in prayer. If I make a demand, may it be only of myself.

Max Lucado

God's Promise of Love

His banner over me was love.

Song of Solomon 2:4 KJV

In the Bible, God makes this amazing promise—He promises that He loves you.

And it's a promise that He intends to keep.

No matter where you are (and no matter what you've done), you're never beyond the reach of God's love. So take time tonight (and every night) to thank Him for love that is too big to understand with your head, but not too big to feel with your heart.

Sleep On It!

The life of faith is a daily exploration of the constant and countless ways in which God's grace and love are experienced.

Eugene Peterson

Tonight, Here Are Some Big Ideas About Patience

Here are two important ideas. Take a few minutes to talk to your mom or dad about what these quotations mean.

In the Bible, patience is not a passive acceptance of circumstances. It is a courageous perseverance in the face of suffering and difficulty.

Warren Wiersbe

We must learn to wait.
There is grace supplied to the one who waits.

Mrs. Charles E. Cowman

Bedtime Devotional 197

Tonight, Try to Memorize This Verse

I remind you to keep ablaze
the gift of God that is in you.

2 Timothy 1:6 Holman CSB

This is an important Bible verse. Practice saying it several times. And then, talk to your mom or dad about exactly what the verse means . . .

A Tip for Parents

Tonight, talk to your child about . . .
using the gifts God gives.

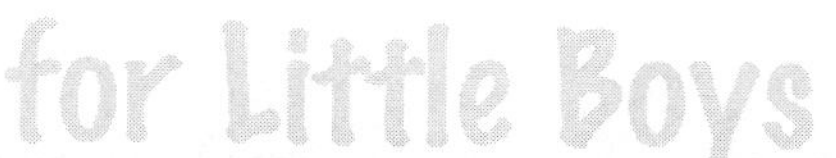

Bedtime Devotional 198

What a Friend!

Just as the Father has loved Me, I have also loved you; abide in My love.

John 15:9 NASB

Do you know that Jesus loves you? And have you thought about exactly what His love should mean to you? Well, Christ's love should make you feel better about your life, your family, your future, and yourself.

There's an old song that says, "What a friend we have in Jesus." Those words are certainly true! When you invite Him into your heart, Jesus will be your friend forever.

Jesus wants you to have a happy, healthy life. He wants you to behave yourself, and He wants you to feel good about yourself. And now, it's up to you to do your best to live up to the hopes and dreams of your very best friend: Jesus.

Sleep On It!

Jesus Christ is the first and last, author and finisher, beginning and end, alpha and omega, and by Him all other things hold together. He must be first or nothing. God never comes next!

Vance Havner

Bedtime Devotional 199

Tonight, Here Are Some Big Ideas About Saying Thanks to God

Here are two important ideas. Take a few minutes to talk to your mom or dad about what these quotations mean.

Praise and thank God for who He is
and for what He has done for you.

Billy Graham

Thank God every morning when you get up that
you have something to do that day which must be done,
whether you like it or not.

Charles Kingsley

Bedtime Devotional 200

Wisdom

Do not deceive yourselves. If any one of you thinks he is wise by the standards of this age, he should become a "fool" so that he may become wise. For the wisdom of this world is foolishness in God's sight.

1 Corinthians 3:18-19 NIV

If you look in a dictionary, you'll see that the word "wisdom" means "using good judgement, and knowing what is true." But there's more: it's not just enough to know what's right; if you really want to become a wise person, you must also do what's right.

A big part of "doing what's right" is learning self-control . . . and the best day to start learning self-control is this one!

Sleep On It!

Need wisdom? Study God's Word and hang out with wise people.

How Would Jesus Behave?

You did not choose Me, but I chose you. I appointed you that you should go out and produce fruit, and that your fruit should remain, so that whatever you ask the Father in My name, He will give you.

John 15:16 Holman CSB

If you're not certain whether something is right or wrong, ask yourself a simple question: "What would Jesus do if He were here?" The answer to that question will tell you how to behave yourself.

Jesus was perfect, but we are not. Still, we must try as hard as we can to be like Him. When we do, we will love others, just like Christ loves us.

Sleep On It!

Want to know what Jesus would do? Then learn what Jesus did!

God Knows Best

However, each one must live his life in the situation the Lord assigned when God called him.

1 Corinthians 7:17 Holman CSB

Here are three things to think about: 1. God loves you. 2. God wants what's best for you. 3. God has a plan for you.

God's plan may not always happen exactly like you want, but remember: God always knows best. Sometimes, even though you may want something very badly, you must still be patient and wait for the right time to get it. And the right time, of course, is determined by God.

Even if you don't get exactly what you want today, you can be sure that God wants what's best for you . . . today, tomorrow, and forever.

Sleep On It!

God has a plan for the world and for you. When you discover His plan for your life—and when you follow in the footsteps of His Son—you will be rewarded. The place where God is leading you is the place where you must go.

Bedtime Devotional 203

Tonight, Here Are Some Big Ideas About Behaving Yourself

Here are two important ideas. Take a few minutes to talk to your mom or dad about what these quotations mean.

> Do nothing that you would not like to be doing when Jesus comes. Go no place where you would not like to be found when He returns.
>
> Corrie ten Boom

> Life is a series of choices between the bad, the good, and the best. Everything depends on how we choose.
>
> Vance Havner

Learning to Share

Be generous: Invest in acts of charity. Charity yields high returns.

Ecclesiastes 11:1 MSG

Lots of people in the world aren't as fortunate as you are. Some of these folks live in faraway places, and that makes it harder to help them. But other people who need your help are living very near you.

Ask your parents to help you find ways to do something nice for folks who need it. And don't forget that everybody needs love, kindness, and respect, so you should always be ready to share those things, too.

Sleep On It!

He climbs highest who helps another up.

Zig Ziglar

Where Does God Fit In?

Every morning he wakes me. He teaches me to listen like a student. The Lord God helps me learn . . .

Isaiah 50:4-5 NCV

Where does God fit in to your life? Do you "squeeze Him in" on Sundays and at mealtimes? Or do you talk to Him more often than that?

Even if you're the busiest kid on the planet, you can still make time for God. And when you think about it, isn't that the very least you should do?

Sleep On It!

We all need to make time for God. Even Jesus made time to be alone with the Father.

Kay Arthur

Bedtime Devotional 206

The Powerful Life

God's Way is not a matter of mere talk; it's an empowered life.

1 Corinthians 4:20 MSG

How do people know that you're a Christian? Well, you can tell them, of course. And make no mistake about it: talking about your faith in God is a very good thing to do. But telling people about Jesus isn't enough. You should also show people how a Christian (like you) should behave.

God wants you to be loving and giving. That way, when another person sees how you behave, that person will know what it means to be a good Christian . . . a good Christian like you!

Sleep On It!

Follow a good example and be a good example. Max Lucado writes, "In our faith we follow in someone's steps. In our faith we leave footprints to guide others. It's the principle of discipleship."

Bedtime Devotional 207

Stop Fighting

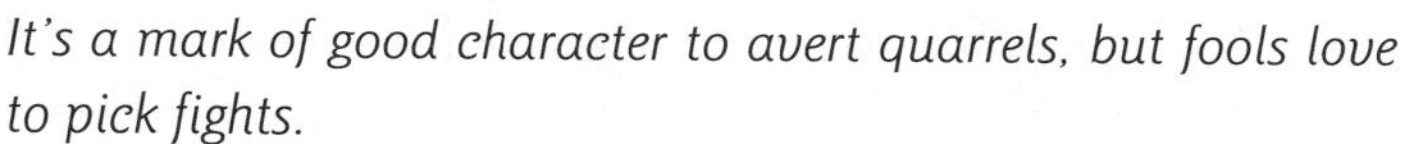

It's a mark of good character to avert quarrels, but fools love to pick fights.

Proverbs 20:3 MSG

Since the days of Cain and Abel, people have discovered plenty of things to fight about (Cain and Abel, by the way, were the sons of Adam and Eve). It seems that fighting is a favorite activity for many people, even though it's almost always the wrong thing to do.

Kids should do their best to avoid fights, period. So do yourself a favor: try to avoid senseless scuffles, foolish fights, alarming arguments, and constant conflicts. You'll be glad you did . . . and so will God.

Sleep On It!

Tempted to fight? Walk away. The best fights are those that never happen.

Bedtime Devotional 208

Don't Grow Tired of Forgiving

Then Peter came to him and asked, "Lord, how often should I forgive someone who sins against me? Seven times?" "No!" Jesus replied, "seventy times seven!"

Matthew 18:21-22 NLT

How often does God forgive us? More times than we can count! And that, by the way, is exactly how many times that God expects us to forgive other people—more times than we care to count.

Of this you can be sure: God won't ever get tired of forgiving you. And, because He has forgiven you, He doesn't want you to get tired of forgiving other people . . . ever!

Sleep On It!

The time to forgive is now! God wants you to forgive people now, not later. Why? Because God knows that it's the right thing to do. And, of course, God wants you to be happy, not angry. God knows what's best for you, so if you have somebody you need to forgive, do it now.

Bedtime Devotional 209

Tonight, Try to Memorize This Verse

May the words of my mouth
and the meditation of my heart
be pleasing in your sight, O LORD,
my Rock and my Redeemer.

Psalm 19:14 NIV

This is an important Bible verse. Practice saying it several times. And then, talk to your mom or dad about exactly what the verse means . . .

A Tip for Parents

Tonight, talk to your child about . . .
pleasing God.

Tonight, Here Are Some Big Ideas About Kindness

Here are two important ideas. Take a few minutes to talk to your mom or dad about what these quotations mean.

> The attitude of kindness is everyday stuff
> like a great pair of sneakers. Not frilly. Not fancy.
> Just plain and comfortable.
>
> Barbara Johnson

> Keep your eyes open wide and your heart open wider.
>
> Criswell Freeman

Real Love

For the LORD your God has arrived to live among you. He is a mighty savior. He will rejoice over you with great gladness. With his love, he will calm all your fears. He will exult over you by singing a happy song.

Zephaniah 3:17 NLT

How big is God's love for you? As long as you're alive, you'll never be able to figure it out because God's love is just too big to understand. But this much we know: God loves you so much that He sent His Son Jesus to come to this earth so you could live forever in heaven.

God's love is bigger and more powerful than anybody can imagine, but His love is very real. So do yourself a favor right now: accept God's love with open arms and welcome His Son Jesus into your heart. When you do, your life will be changed today, tomorrow, and forever.

Sleep On It!

Remember: It's not enough to talk about being a Christian; you must also show other people that you're a disciple of Christ.

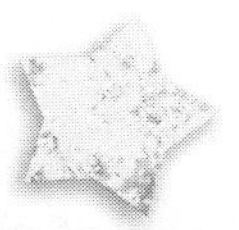

Bedtime Devotional 212

Promises You Can Trust

Do not be afraid or discouraged. For the LORD your God is with you wherever you go.

Joshua 1:9 NLT

God has made quite a few promises to you, and He intends to keep every single one of them. You will find these promises in a book like no other: the Holy Bible. The Bible is your map for life here on earth and for life in heaven.

God's promises never fail and they never grow old. You must trust those promises and share them with your family, with your friends, and with the world . . . starting now . . . and ending never.

Sleep On It!

God keeps His promises to you, so make sure that you keep your promises to Him.

Pay Attention to Your Bible

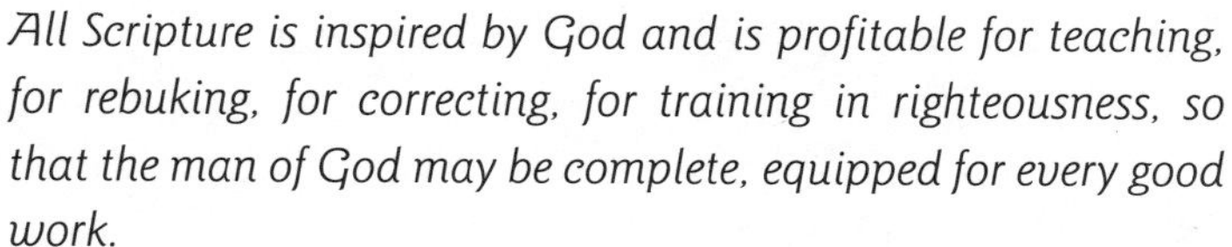

All Scripture is inspired by God and is profitable for teaching, for rebuking, for correcting, for training in righteousness, so that the man of God may be complete, equipped for every good work.

2 Timothy 3:16-17 Holman CSB

Do you think about the Bible a lot . . . or not? Hopefully, you pay careful attention to the things you learn from God's Word! After all, the Bible is God's message to you. It's not just a book, it's a priceless, one-of-a-kind treasure . . . and it has amazing things to teach you. So start learning about the Bible now, and keep learning about it for as long as you live!

Sleep On It!

Who's supposed to be taking care of your Bible? If it's you, then take very good care of it; it's by far the most important book you own!

Developing New Habits

For every tree is known by its own fruit.

Luke 6:44 NKJV

Perhaps you've tried to become a more patient person, but you're still falling back into your old habits. If so, don't get discouraged. Instead, become even more determined to become the person God wants you to be.

If you trust God, and if you keep asking Him to help you change bad habits, He will help you make yourself into a new person. So, if at first you don't succeed, keep praying. If you keep asking, you'll eventually get the answers you need.

Sleep On It!

Choose your habits carefully: habits are easier to make than they are to break, so be careful!

Tonight, Try to Memorize This Verse

For I know the plans I have for you,
declares the LORD,
plans to prosper you and not to harm you,
plans to give you hope and a future.

Jeremiah 29:11 NIV

This is an important Bible verse. Practice saying it several times. And then, talk to your mom or dad about exactly what the verse means . . .

A Tip for Parents

Tonight, talk to your child about . . .
God's plan.

Bedtime Devotional 216

Think About What's Right

Keep your eyes focused on what is right. Keep looking straight ahead to what is good.

Proverbs 4:25 ICB

In the Book of Proverbs, King Solomon gave us wonderful advice for living wisely. Solomon said that we should keep our eyes "focused on what is right." In other words, we should do our best to say and do the things that we know are pleasing to God.

The next time you're tempted to say an unkind word or to say something that isn't true, remember the advice of King Solomon. Solomon knew that it's always better to do the right thing, even when it's tempting to do otherwise. So if you know something is wrong, don't do it; instead, do what you know to be right. When you do, you'll be saving yourself a lot of trouble and you'll be obeying the Word of God.

Sleep On It!

If your friends try to convince you to misbehave, say no! You'll feel better about yourself when you do.

Bedtime Devotional 217

The Kid in the Mirror

For you made us only a little lower than God, and you crowned us with glory and honor.

Psalm 8:5 NLT

Do you really like the person you see when you look into the mirror? You should! After all, the person in the mirror is a very special person who is made—and loved—by God.

In fact, you are loved in many, many ways: God loves you, your parents love you, and your family loves you, for starters. So you should love yourself, too.

So here's something to think about: since God thinks you're special, and since so many people think you're special, isn't it about time for you to agree with them? Of course it is! It's time to say, "You're very wonderful and very special," to the person you see in the mirror.

Sleep On It!

God loves you . . . and you should too.

You Feel Better About Yourself When You Share

Be generous to the poor—you'll never go hungry; shut your eyes to their needs, and run a gauntlet of curses.

Proverbs 28:27 MSG

The more you share, the quicker you'll discover this fact: Good things happen to people (like you) who are kind enough to share the blessings that God has given them.

Sharing makes you feel better about yourself. Whether you're at home or at school, remember that the best rewards go to the kids who are kind and generous—not to the people who are unkind or stingy. So do what's right: share. You'll feel lots better about yourself when you do.

Sleep On It!

When somebody needs a helping hand, he doesn't need it tomorrow or the next day. He needs it now, and that's exactly when you should offer to help. Good deeds, if they are really good, happen sooner rather than later.

Marie T. Freeman

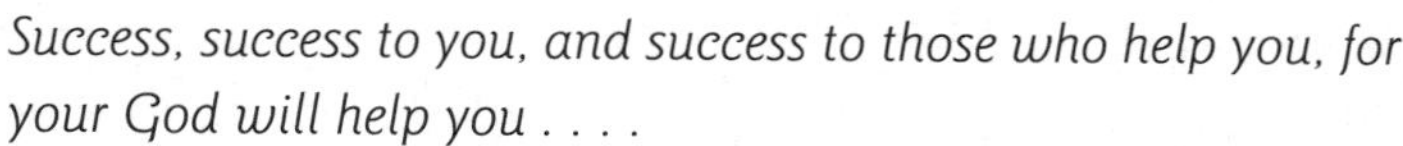

Success, success to you, and success to those who help you, for your God will help you . . . .

I Chronicles 12:18 NIV

God makes this promise: If you have faith in Him, you can do BIG things! So if you have something important to do, pray about it and ask God for help. When you ask God to help you, He will. And while you're at it, never be afraid to ask your parents for help.

When you talk things over with your parents, you'll soon discover that they want you to do BIG things . . . and they can give you LOTS of help.

Sleep On It!

Success and happiness are not destinations. They are exciting, never-ending journeys.

Zig Ziglar

Trusting God

"I say this because I know what I am planning for you," says the Lord. "I have good plans for you, not plans to hurt you. I will give you hope and a good future."

Jeremiah 29:11 NCV

Sometimes, things happen that we simply don't understand. And that's exactly how God intends it! You see God has given us many gifts, but He hasn't given us the power to understand everything that happens in our world (that comes later, when we get to heaven!).

The Bible tells us God's plans are far bigger than we humans can possibly understand. That's one of the reasons that God doesn't make His plans clear to us. But even when we can't understand why God allows certain things to happen, we can trust His love for us.

The Bible does make one part of God's plan perfectly clear: we should accept His Son Jesus into our hearts so that we might have eternal life (John 3:16). And when we do, we are protected today, tomorrow, and forever.

Sleep On It!

God has very big plans in store for your life, so trust Him and wait patiently for those plans to unfold. And remember: God's timing is best.

Honesty Pays

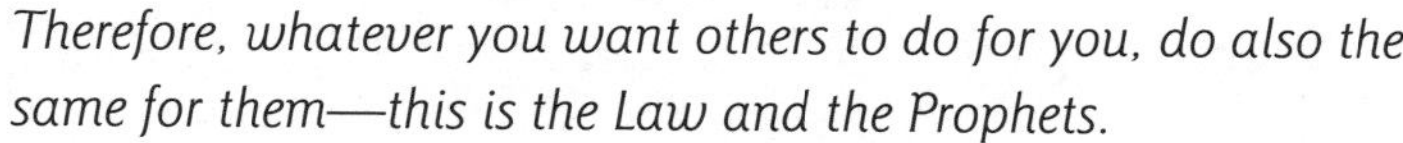

Therefore, whatever you want others to do for you, do also the same for them—this is the Law and the Prophets.

Matthew 7:12 Holman CSB

Do you want other people to be honest with you? Of course you do. And that's why you should be honest with them. The words of Matthew 7:12 remind us that, as believers in Christ, we should treat others as we wish to be treated. And that means telling them the truth!

The Golden Rule is your tool for deciding how you will treat other people. When you use the Golden Rule as your guide for living, your words and your actions will be pleasing to other people and to God.

Sleep On It!

It is important to treat everybody with respect and kindness. And that means everybody!

Tonight, Try to Memorize This Verse

But the fruit of the Spirit is love, joy,
peace, patience, kindness, goodness,
faith, gentleness, self-control.
Against such things there is no law.

Galatians 5:22-23 Holman CSB

This is an important Bible verse. Practice saying it several times. And then, talk to your mom or dad about exactly what the verse means . . .

A Tip for Parents

Tonight, talk to your child about . . .
the fruits of the Spirit.

God's Greatest Promise

I assure you: Anyone who believes has eternal life.

John 6:47 Holman CSB

It's time to remind yourself of a promise that God made a long time ago—the promise that God sent His Son Jesus to save the world and to save you! And when you stop to think about it, there can be no greater promise than that.

No matter where you are, God is with you. God loves you, and He sent His Son so that you can live forever in heaven with your loved ones. WOW! That's the greatest promise in the history of the universe. The End.

Sleep On It!

God's gift of eternal life is amazing. Talk to your friends about God's promise of eternal life, and what that promise means to you.

Bedtime Devotional 224

A GREAT BIG THANK YOU

Praise the LORD. Give thanks to the LORD, for he is good; his love endures forever.

Psalm 106:1 NIV

If you're like most boys, you're very busy doing things and learning things. But no matter how busy you are—even if you hardly have a moment to spare—you should still slow down and say "Thank You," to God!

God has given you many things, and you owe Him everything, including a GREAT BIG THANK YOU, starting now (and ending never!).

Sleep On It!

Whether it's daytime or nighttime, it's always the right time to praise God.

Listen to Your Parents

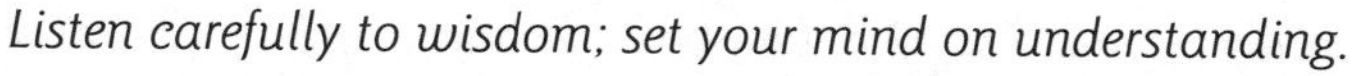

Listen carefully to wisdom; set your mind on understanding.

Proverbs 2:2 NCV

Are you the kind of boy who listens carefully to the things your parents tell you? You should. Your parents want the very best for you. They want you to be happy and healthy; they want you to be smart and to do smart things. Your parents have much to teach you, and you have much to learn. So listen carefully to the things your mom and dad have to say. And ask lots of questions. When you do, you'll soon discover that your parents have lots of answers . . . lots of very good answers.

Sleep On It!

Listening is loving.

Zig Ziglar

God Teaches Us

If you hide your sins, you will not succeed. If you confess and reject them, you will receive mercy.

Proverbs 28:13 NCV

The Bible says that when people make mistakes, God corrects them. And that means that if you make a mistake, God will try to find a way to teach you how to keep from making that same mistake again.

God doesn't expect you to be perfect, but He does expect you to learn from your mistakes—NOW!

Sleep On It!

When you make a mistake, learn something and forgive someone: yourself. Remember, you don't have to be perfect to be wonderful.

Bedtime Devotional 227

The Best Time to Be Obedient

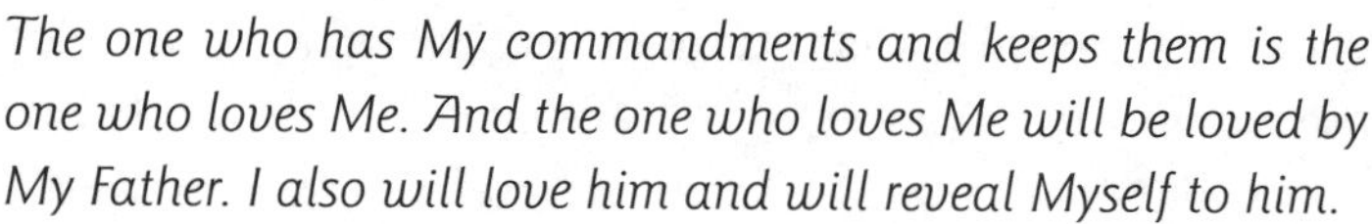

The one who has My commandments and keeps them is the one who loves Me. And the one who loves Me will be loved by My Father. I also will love him and will reveal Myself to him.

John 14:21 Holman CSB

When is the best time to be obedient? It's always the right time to obey your parents, your teachers, and your Father in heaven.

It's not enough to know what's right; if you really want to become a better person, you must also do what's right. Starting now, and stopping never.

Sleep On It!

Stay away from places where you might be easily tempted to disobey God.

Patience and the Golden Rule

Always be humble and gentle. Be patient and accept each other with love.

Ephesians 4:2 ICB

Jesus gave us a Golden Rule for living: He said that we should treat other people in the same way that we want to be treated. And because we want other people to be patient with us, we, in turn, must be patient with them.

Being patient with other people means treating them with kindness, respect, and understanding. It means waiting our turn when we're standing in line and forgiving our friends when they've done something we don't like. Sometimes, it's hard to be patient, but we've got to do our best. And when we do, we're following the Golden Rule—God's rule for how to treat others—and everybody wins!

Sleep On It!

Patience pays; recklessness doesn't.

When Friends Misbehave

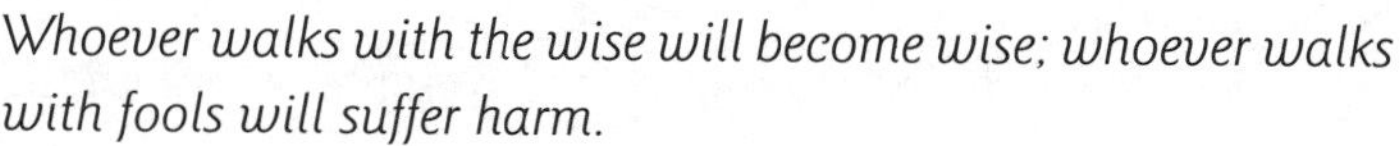

Whoever walks with the wise will become wise; whoever walks with fools will suffer harm.

Proverbs 13:20 NLT

If you're like most people, you have probably been tempted to "go along with the crowd" . . . even when the crowd was misbehaving. But here's something to think about: just because your friends may be misbehaving doesn't mean that you have to misbehave, too.

When people behave badly, they can spoil things in a hurry. So make sure that they don't spoil things for you.

So, if your friends misbehave, don't copy them! Instead, do the right thing. You'll be glad you did . . . and so will God!

Sleep On It!

Remember that it's more important to be respected than to be liked.

Bedtime Devotional 230

Finish What You Begin

We say they are happy because they did not give up. You have heard about Job's patience, and you know the Lord's purpose for him in the end. You know the Lord is full of mercy and is kind.

James 5:11 NCV

Jesus finished what He began, and so should you. Jesus didn't give in, and neither should you. Jesus did what was right, and so should you.

Are you facing something that is hard for you to do? If so, you may be tempted to quit. If so, remember this: whatever your problem, God can handle it. Your job is to keep working until He does.

Sleep On It!

If things don't work out at first, don't quit. If you never try, you'll never know how good you can be.

Tonight, Here Are Some Big Ideas About Your Prayers

Here are two important ideas. Take a few minutes to talk to your mom or dad about what these quotations mean.

Take life one day and one prayer at a time.

Stormie Omartian

Prayer accomplishes more than anything else.

Bill Bright

Bedtime Devotional 232

Be Hopeful

We have this hope—like a sure and firm anchor of the soul—that enters the inner sanctuary behind the curtain.

Hebrews 6:19 Holman CSB

Are you a hope-filled boy? Hopefully so!

When you stop to think about it, you have lots of reasons to be hopeful: God loves you, your family loves you, and you've got a very bright future ahead of you. So trust God, and be hopeful. When you do, you'll be a happier person . . . and God will smile.

Sleep On It!

As long as God is in His heaven, there's always hope . . . so don't give up!

Bedtime Devotional 233

Time with God

Careful planning puts you ahead in the long run; hurry and scurry puts you further behind.

Proverbs 21:5 MSG

How much time do you spend getting to know God? A lot? A little? Almost none? Hopefully, you answered, "a lot."

God loved this world so much that He sent His Son to save it. And now only one real question remains for you: what will you do in response to God's love? God deserves your prayers, your obedience, and your love—and He deserves these things all day every day, not just on Sunday mornings.

Sleep On It!

You should plan to spend some time with God every day . . . and you should stick to your plan!

Bedtime Devotional 234

Life Is a Gift

Live full lives, full in the fullness of God. God can do anything, you know—far more than you could ever imagine or guess or request in your wildest dreams! He does it not by pushing us around but by working within us, his Spirit deeply and gently within us.

Ephesians 3:19-20 MSG

Life is a gift from God. A wonderful gift, a glorious gift, an amazing gift. Your job is to unwrap that gift, to use it wisely, and to give thanks to the Giver.

Are you going to treat this day (and every one hereafter) as a special gift to be enjoyed and celebrated? You should—and if you really want to please God, that's exactly what you will do.

Sleep On It!

Life is a glorious opportunity.

Billy Graham

Tonight, Try to Memorize This Verse

Good people's words
will help many others.

Proverbs 10:21 NCV

This is an important Bible verse. Practice saying it several times. And then, talk to your mom or dad about exactly what the verse means . . .

A Tip for Parents

Tonight, talk to your child about . . .
helping others.

Bedtime Devotional 236

Obedience Leads to Happiness

You are young, but do not let anyone treat you as if you were not important. Be an example to show the believers how they should live. Show them with your words, with the way you live, with your love, with your faith, and with your pure life.

1 Timothy 4:12 ICB

Do you want to be happy? Then you should learn to obey your parents and your teachers. And, of course, you should also learn to obey God. When you do, you'll discover that happiness goes hand-in-hand with good behavior.

The happiest people do not misbehave; the happiest people are not cruel or greedy. The happiest people don't disobey their parents, their teachers, or their Father in heaven. The happiest people are those who obey the rules.

And it's up to you to make sure that you're one of those happy people.

Sleep On It!

When should you get tired of obeying God? The answer to that question is simple: Never!

Be Still

Knowing God leads to self-control. Self-control leads to patient endurance, and patient endurance leads to godliness.

2 Peter 1:6 NLT

Sometimes it's hard to sit still, and sometimes it's even harder to be patient! So here's something worth remembering: God wants us to be patient, and we must obey Him or suffer the consequences.

We should be patient with our families, with our friends, and with ourselves . . . especially with ourselves.

Sleep On It!

If you think you're about to say or do something you'll regret later, slow down and take a deep breath, or two deep breaths, or ten, or . . . well you get the idea.

Tonight, Here Are Some Big Ideas About Pleasing God

Here are two important ideas. Take a few minutes to talk to your mom or dad about what these quotations mean.

You must never sacrifice your relationship with God for the sake of a relationship with another person.

Charles Stanley

Make God's will the focus of your life day by day. If you seek to please Him and Him alone, you'll find yourself satisfied with life.

Kay Arthur

Bedtime Devotional 239

You Don't Have to Be Perfect

You're blessed when you're content with just who you are—no more, no less. That's the moment you find yourselves proud owners of everything that can't be bought.

Matthew 5:5 MSG

When God made you, He gave you special talents and opportunities that are yours and yours alone. That means you're a very special, one-of-a-kind person, but that doesn't mean that you should expect to be perfect. After all, only one earthly being ever lived life to perfection, and He was, of course, Jesus. And Jesus loves you even when you're not perfect. Your parents feel the same way. And if all those people love you, you should love yourself, too.

Sleep On It!

The happiest people in the world are not those who have no problems, but the people who have learned to live with those things that are less than perfect.

James Dobson

Need More Patience? Pray About It!

For the eyes of the Lord are over the righteous, and his ears are open unto their prayers: but the face of the Lord is against them that do evil.

1 Peter 3:12 KJV

Would you like to become a more patient person? Then pray about it. Would you like to learn how to use better self-control? Then pray about it. Are you tempted to throw a temper tantrum? Pray about it.

Whenever you pray about something, God hears your prayer . . . and He can help. So don't worry about things; pray about them. God is waiting . . . and listening!

Sleep On It!

Even when prayer does not change your circumstances, prayer is important because it changes you..

Bedtime Devotional 241

Tonight, Try to Memorize This Verse

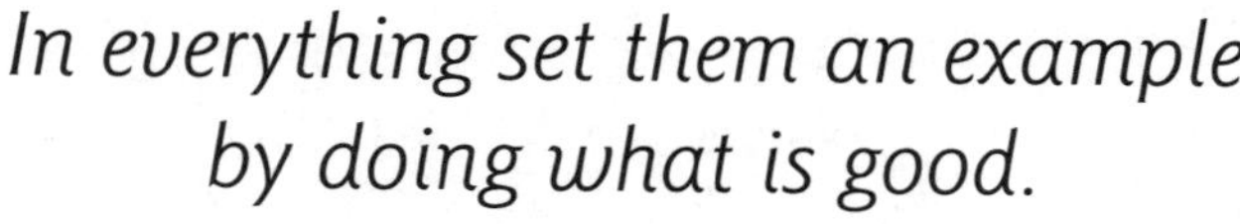

In everything set them an example by doing what is good.

Titus 2:7 NIV

This is an important Bible verse. Practice saying it several times. And then, talk to your mom or dad about exactly what the verse means . . .

A Tip for Parents

Tonight, talk to your child about . . .
setting a good example.

Tonight, Here Are Some Big Ideas About Jesus

Here are two important ideas. Take a few minutes to talk to your mom or dad about what these quotations mean.

What do you think God wants you to do?
The answer is that He wants you to turn to Jesus
and open your life to Him.

Billy Graham

The Bread of Life never gets stale.

Anonymous

Bedtime Devotional 243

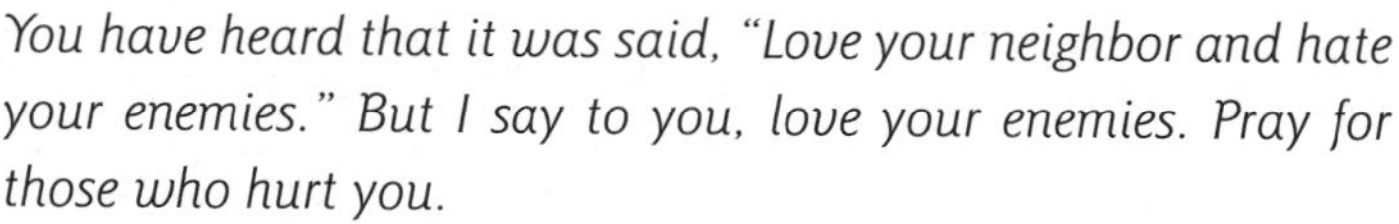

Keep On Forgiving

You have heard that it was said, "Love your neighbor and hate your enemies." But I say to you, love your enemies. Pray for those who hurt you.

Matthew 5:43–44 NCV

If you forgive somebody once, that's enough, right? WRONG!!! Even if you've forgiven somebody many times before, you must keep on forgiving.

Jesus teaches us that we must keep forgiving people even if they continue to misbehave. Why? Because we, too, need to be forgiven over and over again. And if God keeps forgiving us, then we must be willing to do the same thing for others.

Sleep On It!

We must not only learn how to forgive; we must also learn how to keep forgiving. One-time forgiveness is really no forgiveness at all.

Criswell Freeman

Bedtime Devotional 244

Friends You Can Trust

Friends come and friends go, but a true friend sticks by you like family.

Proverbs 18:24 MSG

All lasting friendships are built upon both honesty and trust. Without trust, friends soon drift apart. But with trust, friends can stay friends for a lifetime.

As Christians, we should always try to be trustworthy friends. And, we should be thankful for the people who are loyal friends to us. When we treat other people with honesty and respect, we not only make more friends, but we also keep the friendships we've already made.

Do you want friends you can trust? Then start by being a friend they can trust. That's the way to make your friendships strong, stronger, and strongest!

Sleep On It!

You make friends by being a friend. And when you choose your friends, choose wisely.

Bedtime Devotional 245

When to Stop Temper Tantrums

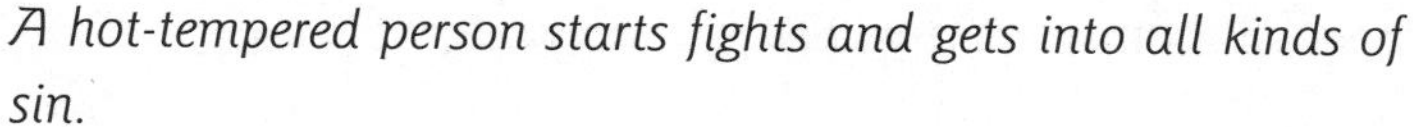

A hot-tempered person starts fights and gets into all kinds of sin.

Proverbs 29:22 NLT

Temper tantrums are one of the silliest ways to lose self-control. Why? Because when we lose our temper, we say things that we shouldn't say, and we do things that we shouldn't do. And to make matters worse, once the tantrum is over, we usually feel embarrassed or worse.

The Bible tells us that it isn't very smart to become angry. That's why we should learn to stop temper tantrums before they get started.

Sleep On It!

If you become angry, the time to step away from the situation is before you say unkind words or do unkind things—not after. So it's perfectly okay to place yourself in "time out" until you can calm down.

Bedtime Devotional 246

No Secrets

The eyes of the Lord are in every place, keeping watch . . . .

Proverbs 15:3 NKJV

Even when nobody else is watching, God is. Nothing that we say or do escapes the watchful eye of our Lord. God understands that we are not perfect, but He also wants us to live according to His rules, not our own.

The next time that you're tempted to say something that you shouldn't say or to do something that you shouldn't do, remember that you can't keep secrets from God. So don't even try!

Sleep On It!

Having trouble hearing God? If so, slow yourself down, tune out the distractions, and listen carefully. God has important things to say; your task is to be still and listen.

Bedtime Devotional 247

Tonight, Try to Memorize This Verse

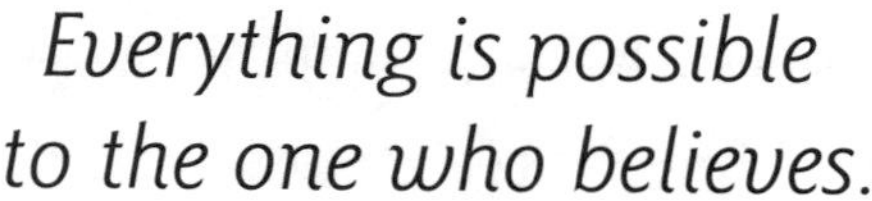

Everything is possible
to the one who believes.

Mark 9:23 Holman CSB

This is an important Bible verse. Practice saying it several times. And then, talk to your mom or dad about exactly what the verse means . . .

A Tip for Parents

Tonight, talk to your child about . . .
the importance of faith.

Be Kind

So rid yourselves of all wickedness, all deceit, hypocrisy, envy, and all slander.

I Peter 2:1 Holman CSB

Do you know what gossip is? It's when we say bad things about people who are not around. When we gossip, we hurt others and we hurt ourselves. That's why the Bible tells us that gossip is wrong.

Sometimes, it's tempting to say bad things about people, and when we do, it makes us feel important . . . for a while. But, after a while, the bad things that we say come back to hurt us, and of course they hurt other people, too.

So if you want to be a kind person and a good friend, don't gossip . . . and don't listen to people who do.

Sleep On It!

Don't say something behind someone's back that you wouldn't say to that person directly.

Bedtime Devotional 249

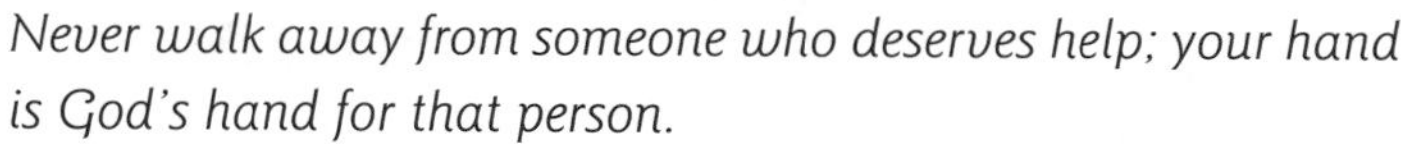

Being a Good Samaritan

Never walk away from someone who deserves help; your hand is God's hand for that person.

Proverbs 3:27 MSG

Sometimes we would like to help make the world a better place, but we're not sure how to do it. Jesus told the story of the "Good Samaritan," a man who helped a fellow traveler when no one else would. We, too, should be good Samaritans when we find people who need our help. A good place to start helping other people is at home or school or church.

Another way that we can help other people is to pray for them. God always hears our prayers, so we should talk with Him as often as we can. When we do, we're not only doing a wonderful thing for the people we pray for, we're also doing a wonderful thing for ourselves, too. Why? Because we feel better about ourselves when we're helping other people.

Sleep On It!

Martin Luther wrote, "Faith never asks whether good works are to be done, but has done them before there is time to ask the question, and it is always doing them." So when in doubt, do something good!

Bedtime Devotional 250

Tonight, Try to Memorize This Verse

The righteous will live by his faith.

Habakkuk 2:4 NIV

This is an important Bible verse. Practice saying it several times. And then, talk to your mom or dad about exactly what the verse means . . .

A Tip for Parents

Tonight, talk to your child about . . .
the need to live by faith.

Bedtime Devotional 251

Look Before You Leap

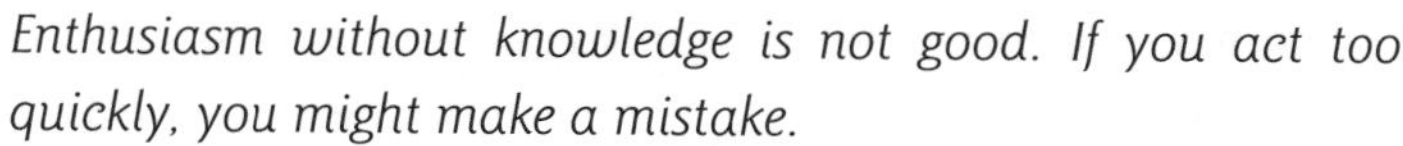

Enthusiasm without knowledge is not good. If you act too quickly, you might make a mistake.

Proverbs 19:2 NCV

Are you sometimes just a little bit impulsive? Do you sometimes fail to look before you leap? If so, God wants you to be a little bit more careful—or maybe a lot more careful!

The Bible makes it clear: we're supposed to behave wisely, not carelessly. But sometimes we're tempted to rush ahead and do things before we think about them.

So do yourself a big favor—slow down, think things through, and look carefully before you leap.

Sleep On It!

No so fast! If you're about to do something, but you're not sure if it's the right thing to do, slow down! It's better to make a good decision than a fast decision.

Bedtime Devotional 252

Only One You

To acquire wisdom is to love oneself; people who cherish understanding will prosper.

Proverbs 19:8 NLT

How many boys in the world are exactly like you? Only one—the boy you see every time you look in the mirror. In other words, the only person in the world who's exactly like you . . . IS YOU! And that means you're special: special to God, special to your family, special to your friends, and a special addition to God's wonderful world!

The Bible says that God made you in "an amazing and wonderful way." So the next time that you start feeling like you don't measure up, remember this: when God made all the people of the earth, He only made one you. And that means you're a V.I.P. And what is a V.I.P.?

A "Very Important Person," of course.

Sleep On It!

God loves you for who you are, not because of the things you've done. So open your heart to God's love . . . when you do, you'll feel better about everything, including yourself.

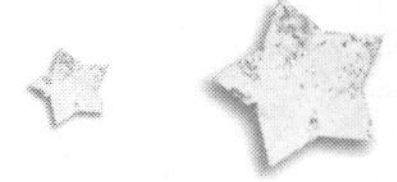

Bedtime Devotional 253

Use Your Ears!

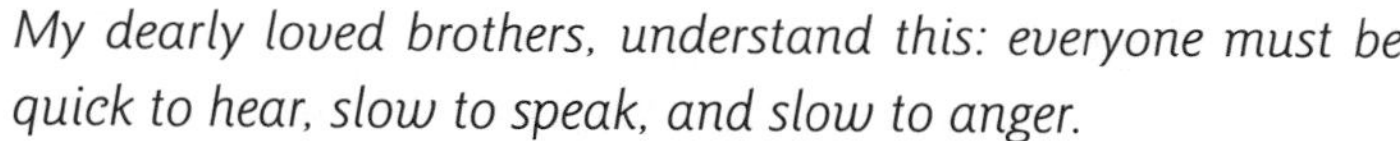

My dearly loved brothers, understand this: everyone must be quick to hear, slow to speak, and slow to anger.

James 1:19 Holman CSB

When God made you, He gave you two ears and one mouth for a very good reason: you can learn at least twice as much by listening as you can by talking. That's why it's usually better to listen first and talk second. But when you're frustrated or tired, it's easy to speak first and think later.

A big part of growing up is learning how to slow down long enough to listen to the things that people have to say. So the next time you're tempted to turn off your ears and tune up your mouth, stop, listen, and think. After all, God gave you two wonderful ears for a very good reason: to use them.

Sleep On It!

Try to listen as much (or more) than you speak.

Bedtime Devotional 254

Don't Judge!

Don't pick on people, jump on their failures, criticize their faults—unless, of course, you want the same treatment. That critical spirit has a way of boomeranging.

Matthew 7:1-2 MSG

Here's something worth thinking about: If you judge other people harshly, God will judge you in the same way. But that's not all (thank goodness!). The Bible also promises that if you forgive other people, you, too, will be forgiven.

Are you tempted to blame people, criticize people, or judge people? If so, remember this: God is already judging what people do, and He doesn't need—or want—your help.

Sleep On It!

God has the wisdom to judge other people, and you don't. So don't be too quick to judge.

Bedtime Devotional 255

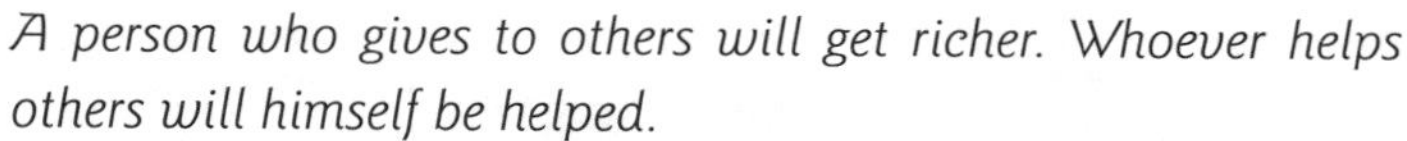

Sharing with Your Family

A person who gives to others will get richer. Whoever helps others will himself be helped.

Proverbs 11:25 ICB

A good place to start sharing is at home—but it isn't always an easy place to start. Sometimes, especially when we're tired or mad, we don't treat our family members as nicely as we should. And that's too bad!

Do you have brothers and sisters? Or cousins? If so, you're lucky.

Sharing your things—without whining or complaining—is a wonderful way to show your family that you love them. So the next time a brother or sister or cousin asks to borrow something, say "yes" without getting mad. It's a great way to say, "I love you."

Sleep On It!

What is your focus today? Joy comes when it is Jesus first, others second . . . then you.

Kay Arthur

Bedtime Devotional 256

Your Amazing Talents!

Now there are varieties of gifts, but the same Spirit. And there are varieties of ministries, and the same Lord.

1 Corinthians 12:4-5 NASB

Face facts: you've got very special talents, talents that have been given to you by God. So here's a question: will you use your talents or not? God wants you to use your talents to become a better person and a better Christian. And that's what you should want for yourself.

As you're trying to figure out exactly what you're good at, be sure and talk about it with your parents. They can help you decide how best to use and improve the gifts God has given you.

Sleep On It!

God gives you talents for a reason: to use them.

Bedtime Devotional 257

Thinking About Your Thoughts

Set your minds on what is above, not on what is on the earth.

Colossians 3:2 Holman CSB

Do you try to think about things that are honorable, true, and pleasing to God? The Bible says that you should. Do you lift your hopes and your prayers to God many times each day? The Bible says that you should. Do you turn away from bad thoughts and bad people? The Bible says that you should.

The Bible instructs you to guard your thoughts against things that are hurtful or wrong. And when you turn away from the bad and turn instead toward God and His Son Jesus, you will be protected and you will be blessed.

Sleep On It!

Good thoughts create good deeds. Good thoughts lead to good deeds and bad thoughts lead elsewhere. So guard your thoughts accordingly.

Bedtime Devotional 258

Tonight, Here Are Some Big Ideas About Waiting Your Turn

Here are two important ideas. Take a few minutes to talk to your mom or dad about what these quotations mean.

If only we could be as patient with other people
as God is with us!

Jim Gallery

God gave everyone patience—
wise people use it.

Anonymous

Bedtime Devotional 259

Real Faith

But whoever keeps His word, truly in him the love of God is perfected. This is how we know we are in Him: the one who says he remains in Him should walk just as He walked.

I John 2:5-6 Holman CSB

Jesus wants to have a real relationship with you. Are you willing to have a real friendship with Him? Unless you can answer this question with a resounding "Yes," you may miss out on some wonderful things.

Every day offers yet another opportunity to behave yourself like a real Christian. When you do, God will guide your steps and bless your endeavors . . . forever.

Sleep On It!

If you're really following Christ, you'll never stay lost for long.

Bedtime Devotional 260

The Gold Standard

Therefore, whatever you want others to do for you, do also the same for them—this is the Law and the Prophets.

Matthew 7:12 Holman CSB

The words of Matthew 7:12 remind us that, as believers in Christ, we should treat others as we wish to be treated. This is called the Golden Rule, but for Christians, it's worth much more than gold.

Do you want other people to forgive you when you make mistakes? Of course you do. And that's why you should be willing to forgive them.

The Golden Rule should be your tool for deciding how you will treat others. So use the Golden Rule as your guide for living and forgiving!

Sleep On It!

When we do little acts of kindness that make life more bearable for someone else, we are walking in love as the Bible commands us.

Barbara Johnson

Inside Out

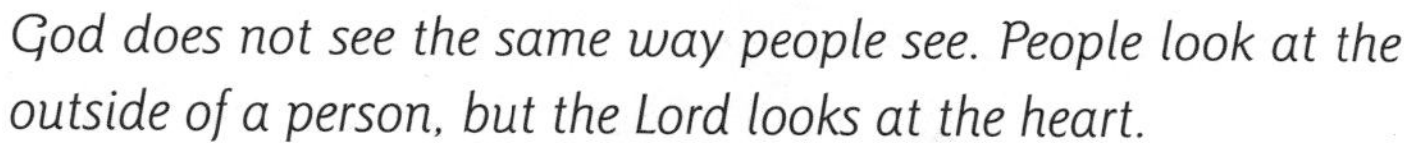

God does not see the same way people see. People look at the outside of a person, but the Lord looks at the heart.

1 Samuel 16:7 NCV

Other people see you from the outside, and sometimes people will judge you by the way you look. But God doesn't care how you look on the outside. Why? Because God is wiser than that; God cares about what you are on the inside—God sees your heart.

If you're like most people, you'll worry a little bit about the way you look (or maybe you worry a lot about it). But please don't worry too much about your appearance!

How you look on the outside isn't important . . . but how you feel on the inside is important. So don't worry about trying to impress other people. Instead of trying to impress other kids, try to impress God by being the best person you can be.

Sleep On It!

Beauty on the outside isn't important . . . beauty on the inside is.

Choices Matter

The thing you should want most is God's kingdom and doing what God wants. Then all these other things you need will be given to you.

Matthew 6:33 NCV

There's really no way to get around it: choices matter. If you make good choices, good things will usually happen to you. And if you make bad choices, bad things will usually happen.

The next time you have an important choice to make, ask yourself this: "Am I doing what God wants me to do?" If you can answer that question with a great big "YES," then go ahead. But if you're not sure if the choice you are about to make is right, slow down. Why? Because choices matter . . . a lot!

Sleep On It!

First you make choices . . . and pretty soon those choices begin to shape your life. That's why you must make smart choices or face the consequences of making dumb ones.

Bedtime Devotional 263

Always the Right Thing to Do

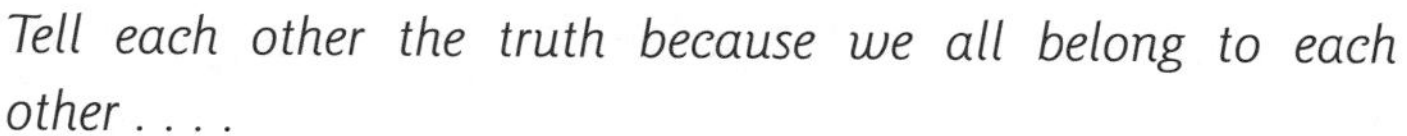

Tell each other the truth because we all belong to each other . . . .

Ephesians 4:25 ICB

It's important to be honest. When you tell the truth, you'll feel better about yourself, and other people will feel better about you, too. But that's not all. When you tell the truth, God knows—and He will reward you for your honesty.

Telling the truth is hard sometimes. But it's better to be honest, even when it's hard. So remember this: telling the truth is always the right thing to do . . . always.

Sleep On It!

Sometimes, we're tempted to tell "little white lies." Unfortunately, little white lies have a tendency to turn black, and they grow. So it's a good idea to avoid untruths of all sizes and colors.

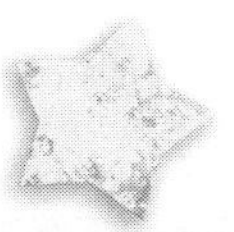

Bedtime Devotional 264

Lessons You Can Learn

Remember what you are taught. And listen carefully to words of knowledge.

Proverbs 23:12 ICB

You can learn a lot about life by paying attention to the things that happen around you . . . and that's exactly what God wants you to do. God is trying to teach you things, and you can learn those things the easy way (by paying attention and obeying God's rules) or the hard way (by making the same mistakes over and over again until you finally learn something from them). Of course, it's better to learn things sooner rather than later . . . starting now.

Sleep On It!

While it is wise to learn from experience, it is wiser to learn from the experience of others.

Rick Warren

Tonight, Here Are Some Big Ideas About Prayer

Here are two important ideas. Take a few minutes to talk to your mom or dad about what these quotations mean.

Don't be overwhelmed . . .
take it one day and one prayer at a time.

Stormie Omartian

Just as our faith strengthens our prayer life,
so do our prayers deepen our faith. Let us pray often,
starting today, for a deeper, more powerful faith.

Shirley Dobson

Bedtime Devotional 266

Obeying Your Parents

We must obey God rather than men.

Acts 5:29 NASB

When your parents ask you to do something, do you usually obey them or do you usually ignore them? When your parents try to get your attention, do you listen or not? When your parents make rules, do you obey those rules or do you break them? Hopefully, you've learned to listen to your parents and to obey.

In order to be an obedient person, you must first learn how to control yourself—otherwise, you won't be able to behave yourself even if you want to. Controlling yourself means that you must slow down long enough to listen to your parents, and then you must be willing to do something about the things your parents tell you to do.

When you learn the importance of obedience, you'll soon discover that good things happen when you behave yourself. And the sooner you learn to listen and to obey, the sooner those good things will start happening . . . to you!

Sleep On It!

When you obey your parents . . . you're pleasing God, and you're doing yourself a BIG favor.

Anger Leads to Trouble

Patience is better than strength.

Proverbs 16:32 ICB

In the Book of Proverbs, King Solomon gave us wonderful advice for living wisely. Solomon warned that impatience and anger lead only to trouble. And he was right!

The next time you're tempted to say an unkind word or to throw a temper tantrum, remember Solomon. He was one of the wisest men who ever lived, and he knew that it's always better to be patient. So remain calm and remember that patience is best. After all, if it's good enough for a wise man like Solomon, it should be good enough for us, too.

Sleep On It!

God and your parents have been patient with you. Now it's your turn to be patient with others.

Bedtime Devotional 268

Pleasing God Is More Important Than Pleasing Friends

For am I now trying to win the favor of people, or God? Or am I striving to please people? If I were still trying to please people, I would not be a slave of Christ.

Galatians 1:10 Holman CSB

Are you a people-pleaser or a God-pleaser? Hopefully, you're far more concerned with pleasing God than you are with pleasing your friends. But face facts: even if you're a devoted Christian, you're still going to feel the urge to impress your friends—and sometimes that urge will be strong.

Here's your choice: you can choose to please God first, or you can fall victim to peer pressure. The choice is yours—and so are the consequences.

Sleep On It!

Make up your mind to find friends who will help you become a better person.

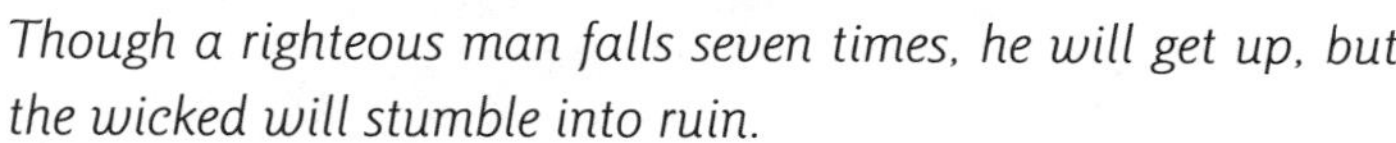

Though a righteous man falls seven times, he will get up, but the wicked will stumble into ruin.

Proverbs 24:16 Holman CSB

If you think you can do something, then you can probably do it. If you think you can't do something, then you probably won't do it.

So remember this: if you're having a little trouble getting something done, don't get mad, don't get frustrated, don't get discouraged, and don't give up. Just keep trying . . . and believe in yourself.

When you try hard—and keep trying hard—you can really do amazing things . . . but if you quit at the first sign of trouble, you'll miss out. So here's a good rule to follow: when you have something that you want to finish, finish it . . . and finish it sooner rather than later.

Sleep On It!

If you give up at the first sign of trouble, you won't do very much. But if you don't give up, you'll become a real winner.

Bedtime Devotional 270

Tonight, Here Are Some Big Ideas About Serving Other People

Here are two important ideas. Take a few minutes to talk to your mom or dad about what these quotations mean.

> God will open up places of service for you
> as He sees you are ready. Meanwhile, study the Bible
> and give yourself a chance to grow.
>
> Warren Wiersbe

> There are times when we are called to love,
> expecting nothing in return. There are times when we are
> called to give money to people who will never say thanks,
> to forgive those who won't forgive us, to come early and
> stay late when no one else notices.
>
> Max Lucado

Joyful Abundance

Shout with joy to the LORD, O earth! Worship the LORD with gladness. Come before him, singing with joy.

Psalm 100:1-2 NLT

Have you made the choice to rejoice? Hopefully so. After all, if you're a Christian, you have plenty of reasons to be joyful.

So today, think about this: God has given you too many blessings to count, but you can certainly count some of those blessings. Your job is to honor God with your prayers, your words, your behavior, and your joy.

Sleep On It!

According to Jesus, it is God's will that His children be filled with the joy of life.

Catherine Marshall

The Best Time to Praise God

The LORD is my strength and song, and He has become my salvation; He is my God, and I will praise Him.

Exodus 15:2 NIV

When is the best time to praise God? In church? Before dinner is served? At bedtime? None of the above. The best time to praise God is all day, every day, to the greatest extent we can, with thanksgiving in our hearts, and with a song on our lips. Dr. Wayne Oates once admitted, "Many of my prayers are made with my eyes open. You see, it seems I'm always praying about something, and it's not always convenient—or safe—to close my eyes." Dr. Oates understood that God always hears our prayers and that the position of our eyelids is of no concern to Him.

So, find a little more time to lift your concerns to God in prayer, and praise Him for all that He has done. Whether your eyes are open or closed, He's listening.

Sleep On It!

Make it a habit to praise God many times each day. God is with you all day long, and you should praise Him all day long.

A Helping Hand

Hatred stirs up trouble, but love forgives all wrongs.

Proverbs 10:12 NCV

Sometimes, young people can be very mean. They can make fun of other people, and when they do so, it's wrong. Period.

As Christians, we should be kind to everyone. And, if other kids say unkind things to a child or make fun of him or her, it's up to us to step in, like the Good Samaritan, and lend a helping hand.

So be a boy who is known for your kindness, not for your cruelty. That's how God wants you to behave. Period.

Sleep On It!

Stand up for what's right! If one of your friends is being cruel, unkind, or discourteous, don't join in! Instead, stand up for the people who need your help. Remember what Jesus said: when you help people in need, you're helping Him, too (Matthew 25:40).

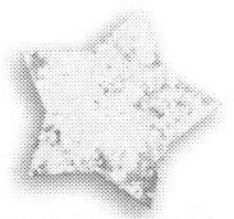

Bedtime Devotional 274

Hit a Home Run

Don't be afraid. Only believe.

Mark 5:36 Holman CSB

His fans called him the "Sultan of Swat." He was Babe Ruth, the baseball player who set records for home runs and strikeouts. Babe's philosophy was simple. He said, "Never let the fear of striking out get in your way." That's smart advice on the diamond or off.

Of course it's never wise to take foolish risks (so buckle up, slow down, and don't do anything stupid!). But when it comes to the game of life, you should not let the fear of failure keep you from taking your swings.

Sleep On It!

Success or failure can be pretty well predicted by the degree to which the heart is fully in it.

John Eldredge

Bedtime Devotional 275

In His Footsteps

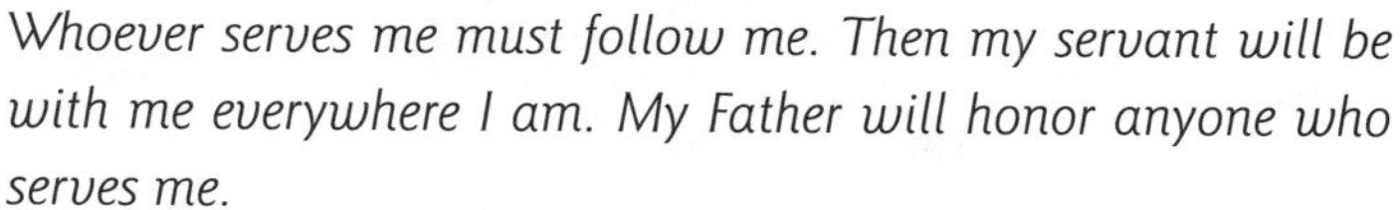

Whoever serves me must follow me. Then my servant will be with me everywhere I am. My Father will honor anyone who serves me.

John 12:26 NCV

Jesus walks with you. Are you walking with Him? Hopefully, you will choose to walk with Him tonight, tomorrow, and every day of your life.

Jesus has called upon believers of every generation (and that includes you) to follow in His footsteps. Will you follow? Please answer that question with a GREAT BIG YES. When you do, your heart will be filled with a GREAT BIG LOVE for Him!

Sleep On It!

Salvation is not a cafeteria where you take what you want and leave the rest. You cannot take Christ as Savior and refuse Him as Lord.

Vance Havner

Bedtime Devotional 276

Pray for Everybody

Hatred stirs up trouble, but love forgives all wrongs.

Proverbs 10:12 NCV

It's usually pretty easy to pray for your friends and family members—all you have to do is find the time. But when it comes to praying for people who have hurt you, well that's a different matter entirely!

Like it or not, God says that you've got to pray for the folks you like and for the folks you don't like. Why? Well maybe it's because God knows that He has already forgiven you, and now He thinks it's about time for you to forgive them.

Sleep On It!

Only the truly forgiven are truly forgiving.

C. S. Lewis

Bedtime Devotional 277

Laugh Whenever You Can

A joyful heart is good medicine . . . .

Proverbs 17:22 Holman CSB

Sometimes, we may feel guilty about having fun when some people around the world are not having any fun at all. But God doesn't want us to spend our lives moping around with frowns on our faces. Far from it! God tells us that a happy heart is a very good thing to have.

So if you're afraid to laugh out loud, don't be. Remember that God wouldn't have given you the gift of laughter if He hadn't intended for you to use it. And remember: if you're laughing, that does not mean that you're unconcerned about people who may be hurting. It simply means that you've taken a little time to have fun, and that's good because God wants you to have a cheerful heart.

Sleep On It!

Whence comes this idea that if what we are doing is fun, it can't be God's will? The God who made giraffes, a baby's fingernails, a puppy's tail, a crooknecked squash, the bobwhite's call, and a young girl's giggle, has a sense of humor. Make no mistake about that.

Catherine Marshall

Bedtime Devotional 278

God Loves to Forgive

If we claim that we're free of sin, we're only fooling ourselves. A claim like that is errant nonsense. On the other hand, if we admit our sins—make a clean breast of them—he won't let us down; he'll be true to himself. He'll forgive our sins and purge us of all wrongdoing.

I John 1:8-9 MSG

Are you perfect? Of course not! Even if you're a very good boy, you're bound to make mistakes.

When you make a mistake, you must try your best to learn from it (so that you won't make the very same mistake again). And, if you have hurt someone—or if you have disobeyed God—you must ask for forgiveness. And here's the good news: when you ask for God's forgiveness, He will always give it. God forgives you every single time you ask Him to. So ask!

Sleep On It!

Get busy making the world a better place. Now that God has forgiven you, it's time for you to show your gratitude by serving Him.

Bedtime Devotional 279

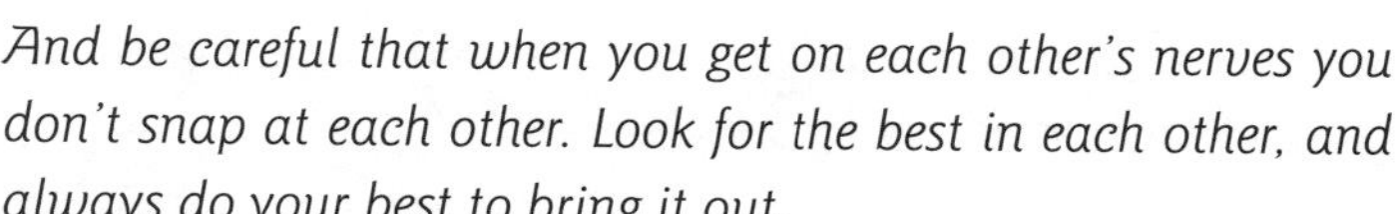

Anger Strikes Out

And be careful that when you get on each other's nerves you don't snap at each other. Look for the best in each other, and always do your best to bring it out.

I Thessalonians 5:15 MSG

The Bible tells us that we should control our tempers. But sometimes, especially when we're angry or frustrated, our words and our actions may not be so gentle. Sometimes, we may say things or do things that are unkind or hurtful to others. When we do, we're wrong.

The next time you're tempted to strike out in anger, don't. And if you want to help your family and friends, remember that kind words are the kind of words you should speak. Always!

Sleep On It!

If you're angry with someone, don't say the first thing that comes to your mind. Instead, catch your breath and start counting until you are once again in control of your temper. If you count to a thousand and you're still counting, go to bed! You'll feel better in the morning.

Bedtime Devotional 280

How to Treat Others

See that no one pays back evil for evil, but always try to do good to each other and to everyone else.

1 Thessalonians 5:15 TLB

Would you like to make the world a better place? If so, you can start by practicing the Golden Rule.

Jesus said, "Whatever you want others to do for you, do also the same for them" (Matthew 7:12 Holman CSB). That means that you should treat other people in the very same way that you want to be treated. That's the Golden Rule.

So here's what you should do: if you want to know how to treat somebody, ask the person you see every time you look into the mirror. The answer you receive will tell you exactly what to do.

Sleep On It!

How would you feel? When you're trying to decide how to treat another person, ask yourself this question: "How would I feel if somebody treated me that way?" Then, treat the other person the way that you would want to be treated.

Bedtime Devotional 281

Always Growing

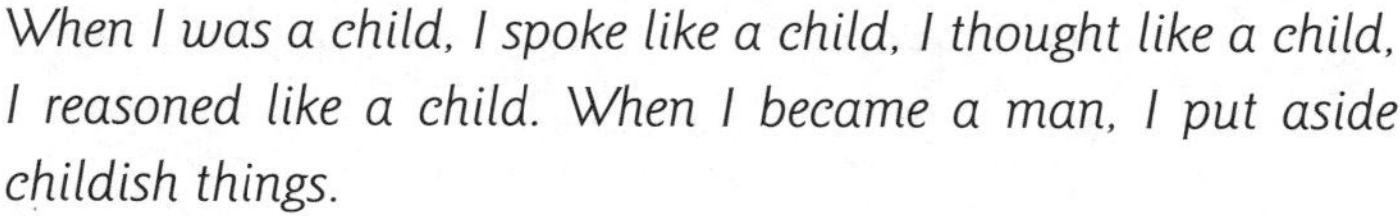

When I was a child, I spoke like a child, I thought like a child, I reasoned like a child. When I became a man, I put aside childish things.

I Corinthians 13:11 Holman CSB

You're growing up day by day, and it's a wonderful thing to watch. Every day, you're learning new things and doing new things. Good for you!

And when should you stop growing up? Hopefully never! That way, you'll always be learning more and doing more.

Do you think it's good to keep growing and growing and growing? If you said "yes," you're right. So remember: you're a very special person today . . . and you'll be just as special when you've grown a little bit more tomorrow.

Sleep On It!

Grown-ups still have plenty to learn . . . and so do you!

Happiness and Honesty

Lead a quiet and peaceable life in all godliness and honesty.

I Timothy 2:2 KJV

Have you ever said something that wasn't true? When you did, were you sorry for what you had said? Probably so.

When we're dishonest, we make ourselves unhappy in surprising ways. Here are just a few troubles that result from dishonesty: we feel guilty and we are usually found out and we disappoint others and we disappoint God. It's easy to see that lies always cause more problems than they solve.

Happiness and honesty always go hand in hand. But it's up to you to make sure that you go hand in hand with them!

Sleep On It!

When telling the truth is hard, it probably means that you're afraid of what others might think—or what they might do—if you're truthful. But even when telling the truth is hard, it's always the right thing to do.

Bedtime Devotional 283

God's Angels

Don't neglect to show hospitality, for by doing this some have welcomed angels as guests without knowing it.

Hebrews 13:2 Holman CSB

The Bible has a lot to say about angels. But maybe you've wondered if angels are really real. If so, wonder no more! If the Bible tells you something, you can be sure that it's true.

The Bible teaches us that angels come from God, so that means they are good and they are helpful. So we don't need to fear angels . . . but neither do we need to pretend that they don't exist!

Sleep On It!

I believe in angels because the Bible says there are angels; and I believe the Bible to be the true Word of God.

Billy Graham

Honesty Is the Right Policy

Therefore laying aside falsehood, speak truth, each one of you, with his neighbor, for we are members of one another.

Ephesians 4:25 NASB

Sometimes people lie, and sometimes they get away with it. But that doesn't mean that it's wise to lie. And that doesn't make lying the right thing to do. Far from it.

Whatever the problem, lying is always a bad solution. And, besides, lying is always against the will of God. So even if other people lie, don't ever believe that they have lied successfully. There's no such thing as a successful lie.

Sleep On It!

When you talk, choose the very same words that you would use if Jesus were looking over your shoulder. Because He is.

Marie T. Freeman

Forgive Other People's Mistakes

I will instruct you and teach you in the way you should go; I will counsel you and watch over you.

Psalm 32:8 NIV

When other people make mistakes, you must find a way to forgive them. And when you make mistakes, as you will from time to time, you must hope that other people will forgive you, too.

When you have done things that you regret, you should apologize, you should clean up the mess you've made, you should learn from your mistakes, and—last but not least—you should forgive yourself. Mistakes happen . . . it's simply a fact of life, and it's simply a part of growing up. So don't be too hard on yourself, especially if you've learned something along the way.

Sleep On It!

Father, take our mistakes and turn them into opportunities.

Max Lucado

Bedtime Devotional 286

Keep Your Eye Upon the Donut

I can do everything through him that gives me strength.

Philippians 4:13 NIV

Here's a poem that was seen many years ago in a small donut shop:

As you travel through life brother,
Whatever be your goal,
Keep your eye upon the donut,
And not upon the hole.

What do you think these words mean? Well, this little poem can teach you an important lesson: You should spend more time looking at the things you have, not worrying about the things you don't have.

When you think about it, you've got more blessings than you can count. So make it a habit to thank God for the gifts He's given you, and don't feel jealous, angry, or sad about all the other stuff.

Sleep On It!

Your attitude toward the future will help create your future.

Bedtime Devotional 287

Making Other People Feel Better

Be gracious in your speech. The goal is to bring out the best in others in a conversation, not put them down, not cut them out.

Colossians 4:6 MSG

Do you like for people to say kind words to you? Of course you do! And that's exactly how other people feel, too. That's why it's so important to say things that make people feel better, not worse.

Your words can help people . . . or not. Make certain that you're the kind of person who says helpful things, not hurtful things. And, make sure that you're the kind of person who helps other people feel better about themselves, not worse.

Sleep On It!

When in doubt, use the Golden Rule to help you decide what to say: If you wouldn't like for somebody to say it about you, don't say it about them!

Bedtime Devotional 288

God Can Handle It

Now the God of all grace, who called you to His eternal glory in Christ Jesus, will personally restore, establish, strengthen, and support you.

I Peter 5:10 Holman CSB

It's a promise that is made over and over again in the Bible: Whatever "it" is, God can handle it.

Life isn't always easy. Far from it! Sometimes, life can be hard, but even then, we're protected by a loving Heavenly Father. When we're worried, God can help us; when we're sad, God can comfort us. God is not just near, He is here. So we should always lift our thoughts and prayers to Him. When we do, He will answer our prayers. Why? Because He is our shepherd, and He has promised to protect us now and forever.

Sleep On It!

When considering the size of your problems, there are two categories that you should never worry about: the problems that are small enough for you to handle, and the ones that aren't too big for God to handle.

Marie T. Freeman

Happy Thoughts

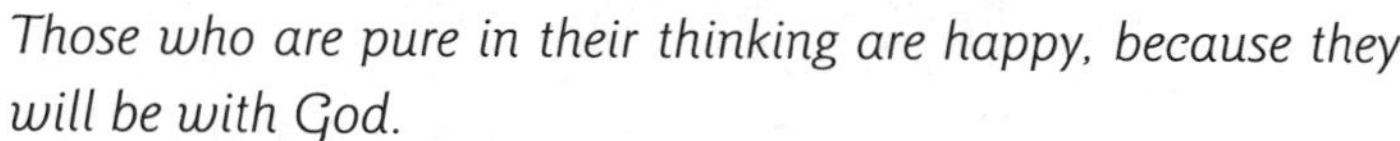

Those who are pure in their thinking are happy, because they will be with God.

Matthew 5:8 NCV

Do you try to think the kind of thoughts that make you happy, not sad? The Bible says that you should. Do you try to think about things that are true and right? The Bible says that you should.

Do you turn away from bad thoughts—and away from people who misbehave? The Bible says that you should.

The Bible instructs you to guard your thoughts against things that are hurtful or wrong. So remember this: when you turn away from the bad thoughts and bad people, you've made a very wise choice.

Sleep On It!

It is important to focus your thoughts on the positive side of life, not the negative side.

Bedtime Devotional 290

Big Rewards When You Do the Right Thing

Do you want to be counted wise, to build a reputation for wisdom? Here's what you do: Live well, live wisely, live humbly. It's the way you live, not the way you talk, that counts.

James 3:13 MSG

If you open up a dictionary, you'll see that the word "wisdom" means "using good judgement, and knowing what is true," But there's more to it than that. It's not enough to know what's right—if you want to be wise, you must also do what's right.

The Bible promises that when you do smart things, you'll earn big rewards, so slow down and think about things before you do them, not after.

Sleep On It!

This is the secret to a lifestyle of worship—doing everything as if you were doing it for Jesus.

Rick Warren

Lies Can Lead to Trouble

Your heart must not be troubled. Believe in God; believe also in Me.

John 14:1 Holman CSB

When we tell a lie, trouble starts. Lots of trouble. But when we tell the truth—and nothing but the truth—we stop Old Man Trouble in his tracks.

When we always tell the truth, we make our worries smaller, not bigger. And that's precisely what God wants us to do.

So, if you'd like to have fewer worries and more happiness, abide by this simple rule: tell the truth, the whole truth, and nothing but the truth. When you do, you'll make many of your worries disappear altogether. And that's the truth!

Sleep On It!

God is bigger than your problems. Whatever worries press upon you today, put them in God's hands and leave them there.

Billy Graham

Tonight, Here Are Some Big Ideas About Forgiveness

Here are two important ideas. Take a few minutes to talk to your mom or dad about what these quotations mean.

There are some facts that will never change.
One fact is that you are forgiven. He sees you better than you see yourself. And that is a glorious fact of your life.

Max Lucado

Is there somebody who's always getting your goat?
Talk to the Shepherd.

Anonymous

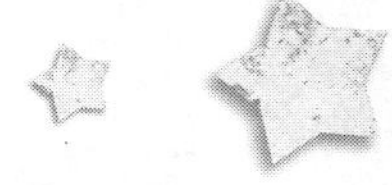

Bedtime Devotional 293

Contentment Now

Keep your lives free from the love of money and be content with what you have, because God has said, "Never will I leave you; never will I forsake you."

Hebrews 13:5 NIV

Where can we find contentment? Is it a result of being wealthy or famous? Nope. Genuine contentment is a gift from God to those who trust Him and follow His commandments.

If we don't find contentment in God, we will never find it anywhere else. But, if we seek Him and obey Him, we will be blessed with joyful, peaceful, meaningful lives. When God dwells at the center of our lives, peace and contentment will belong to us just as surely as we belong to God.

Sleep On It!

God has something wonderful in store for you—and remember that God's timing is perfect—so be patient, trust God, do your best, and expect the best.

Bedtime Devotional 294

A Forever Love

I am the good shepherd. The good shepherd lays down his life for the sheep.

John 10:11 NIV

You've probably heard the song "Jesus Loves Me." And exactly how much does He love you? He loves you so much that He gave His life so that you might live forever with Him in heaven.

How can you repay Christ's love? By accepting Him into your heart and by obeying His rules. When you do, He will love you and bless you today, tomorrow, and forever.

Sleep On It!

Jesus is all compassion. He never betrays us.

Catherine Marshall

Bedtime Devotional 295

An Attitude of Kindness

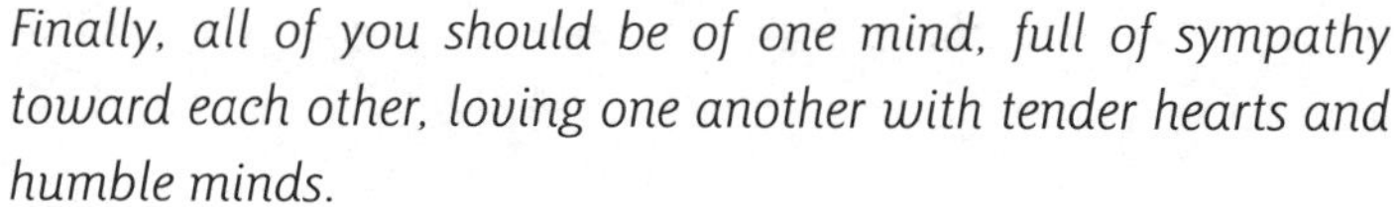

Finally, all of you should be of one mind, full of sympathy toward each other, loving one another with tender hearts and humble minds.

I Peter 3:8 NLT

An attitude of kindness starts in your heart and works its way out from there.

Do you listen to your heart when it tells you to be kind to other people? Hopefully, you do. After all, lots of people in the world aren't as fortunate as you are—and some of these folks are living very near you.

Ask your parents to help you find ways to do nice things for other people. And don't forget that everybody needs love, kindness, and respect, so you should always be ready to share those things, too.

Sleep On It!

There is but one good; that is God. Everything else is good when it looks to Him and bad when it turns from Him.

C. S. Lewis

Bedtime Devotional 296

Listening, to Directions

A fool's way is right in his own eyes, but whoever listens to counsel is wise.

Proverbs 12:15 Holman CSB

Directions, directions, directions. It seems like somebody is always giving you directions: telling you where to go, how to behave, and what to do next. But sometimes all these directions can be confusing! How can you understand everything that everybody tells you? The answer, of course, is that you must pay careful attention to those directions . . . and that means listening.

To become a careful listener, here are some things you must do: 1. Don't talk when you're supposed to be listening (your ears work best when your mouth is closed); 2. Watch the person who's giving the directions (when your eyes and ears work together, it's easier to understand things); 3. If you don't understand something, ask a question (it's better to ask now than to make a mistake later).

Sleep On It!

When you listen to the things other people have to say, it shows that you care about their message and about them. Listening carefully is not just the courteous thing to do, it's also the kind thing to do.

Tonight, Try to Memorize This Verse

Where the Spirit of the Lord is,
there is freedom.

2 Corinthians 3:17 Holman CSB

This is an important Bible verse. Practice saying it several times. And then, talk to your mom or dad about exactly what the verse means . . .

A Tip for Parents

Tonight, talk to your child about . . .
true freedom.

Bedtime Devotional 298

Having Trouble Behaving Yourself? Pray About It!

Rejoice always! Pray constantly. Give thanks in everything, for this is God's will for you in Christ Jesus.

I Thessalonians 5:16-18 Holman CSB

Would you like to become a more obedient boy? Then pray about it. Would you like to learn how to behave yourself a little bit better? Then pray about it. Want to be able to think about things before you get into trouble, not after? Pray for God's help.

If you have questions about whether you should do something or not, pray about it. If there is something you're worried about, ask God to comfort you. And as you pray more, you'll discover that God is always near and that He's always ready to hear from you. So don't worry about things; pray about them. God is waiting to hear from you.

Sleep On It!

When you are praying, your eyes don't always have to be closed. Of course it's good to close your eyes and bow your head, but you can also offer a quick prayer to God with your eyes open. That means that you can pray any time you want.

Bedtime Devotional 299

Questions?

An indecisive man is unstable in all his ways.

James 1:8 Holman CSB

God doesn't explain Himself in ways that we humans would prefer (think about this: if God did explain Himself perfectly, we wouldn't have enough brainpower to understand the explanation that He gave!).

When innocent people are hurt, we question God because we can't figure out exactly what He's doing, or why. But even when we can't answer tough questions like these, we must trust in God's love, God's wisdom, and God's plan.

And while we're waiting for that wonderful day when all our questions will be answered (in heaven), we should use the time that we have here on earth to help the people who need it most.

Sleep On It!

If you're faced with too many questions and too few answers, slow down, and talk to your parents. When you do, you'll discover that your patents probably have more answers than you have questions.

Sometimes Sad

Those people who know they have great spiritual needs are happy, because the kingdom of heaven belongs to them. Those who are sad now are happy, because God will comfort them.

Matthew 5:3-4 NCV

Sometimes, you feel happy, and sometimes you don't. When you're feeling sad, here are two very important things you should do: 1. Talk to your parents about your feelings. 2. Talk to God about your feelings.

Talking with your parents is helpful because your mom and dad understand this: The problems that seem VERY BIG to you today probably won't seem so big tomorrow.

Talking with God helps because God hears your prayers and He helps make things better.

So the next time you're sad, don't hold your feelings inside—talk things over with your parents and with God. When you do, you'll feel better . . . and so will they!

Sleep On It!

God is good, and heaven is forever. These two facts should brighten up even the darkest day.

Marie T. Freeman

Thanking Those Who Serve

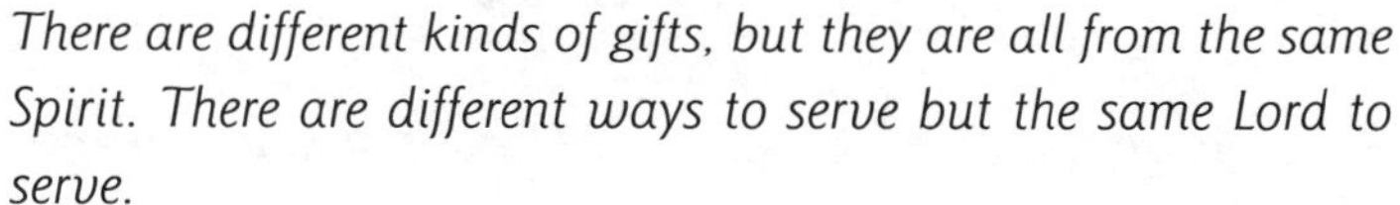

There are different kinds of gifts, but they are all from the same Spirit. There are different ways to serve but the same Lord to serve.

1 Corinthians 12:4–5 NCV

Jesus instructed His disciples to help each other. Those instructions still apply. If we are to be obedient servants of Christ, we must be willing to help those who can't help themselves. In other words, we must become "servants to all."

Some people choose careers that allow them to serve and protect our homes and our world (this includes police officers, firefighters, and those who serve in our military). These brave men and women make very big sacrifices, and we should thank them whenever we can.

So let's all offer prayers of thanks for those brave men and women who serve and protect us . . . and let's all do our best to serve other people wherever we can.

Sleep On It!

Remember the people who live under your roof: Service, like love, should begin at home and work its way out from there.

Everybody Needs to Hear Kind Words

Avoid irreverent, empty speech, for this will produce an even greater measure of godlessness.

2 Timothy 2:16 Holman CSB

Your words can help other people . . . or not. So please make sure that you're the kind of guy who says helpful things, not hurtful things. You'll feel better about yourself when you help other people feel better about themselves.

Do you like for people to say kind words to you? Of course you do! And that's exactly how other people feel, too. That's why it's so important to say things that make people feel better, not worse.

Everybody needs to hear kind words, and that's exactly the kind of words they should hear from you!

Sleep On It!

If you don't know what to say . . . don't say anything. Sometimes, a hug works better than a whole mouthful of words.

Thanks for the Memories

I give thanks to my God for every remembrance of you.

Philippians 1:3 Holman CSB

In his letter to the Philippians, Paul wrote to his distant friends saying that he thanked God every time he remembered them. We, too, should thank God for the family and friends He has brought into our lives.

Today, let's give thanks to God for all the people who love us, for brothers and sisters, parents and grandparents, aunts and uncles, cousins, and friends. And then, as a way of thanking God, let's obey Him by being especially kind to our loved ones. They deserve it, and so does He.

Sleep On It!

The best times in life are made a thousand times better when shared with a dear friend.

Luci Swindoll

God Solves Problems

Since God assured us, "I'll never let you down, never walk off and leave you," we can boldly quote, God is there, ready to help; I'm fearless no matter what. Who or what can get to me?

Hebrews 13:5-6 MSG

Do you have a problem that you haven't been able to solve? Welcome to the club! Life is full of problems that don't have easy solutions. But if you have a problem that you can't solve, there is something you can do: turn that problem over to God. He can handle it.

God has a way of solving our problems if we let Him; our job is to let Him. God can handle things that we can't. And the sooner we turn our concerns over to Him, the sooner He will go to work solving those troubles that are simply too big for us to handle.

If you're worried or discouraged, pray about it. And ask your parents and friends to pray about it, too. And then stop worrying because no problem is too big for God.

Sleep On It!

He is always thinking about us. We are before his eyes. The Lord's eye never sleeps, but is always watching out for our welfare. We are continually on His heart.

C. H. Spurgeon

No Regrets

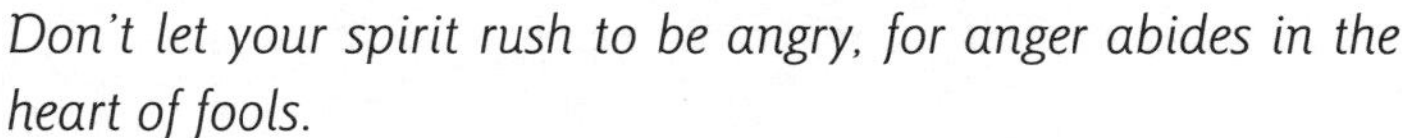

Don't let your spirit rush to be angry, for anger abides in the heart of fools.

Ecclesiastes 7:9 Holman CSB

When you're angry, you will be tempted to say things and do things that you'll regret later. So don't do them! Instead of doing things in a hurry, slow down long enough to calm yourself down.

Jesus does not intend that you strike out against other people, and He doesn't intend that your heart be troubled by anger. Your heart should instead be filled with love, just like Jesus' heart was . . . and is!

Sleep On It!

If you become angry, sometimes it's better to say less, not more. The best time to think about your words is before you speak them, not after.

Who Controls You?

Be imitators of God, therefore, as dearly loved children.

Ephesians 5:1 NIV

Do you try hard to control yourself? If so, that's good because God wants all His children (including you) to behave themselves.

Sometimes, it's hard to be a well-behaved boy, especially if you have friends who don't behave nicely. But if your friends misbehave, don't imitate them. Instead, listen to your conscience, talk to your parents, and do the right thing . . . NOW!

Sleep On It!

Start now! If you really want to become a well-behaved person, the best day to get started is this one.

Listen to Your Conscience

I always do my best to have a clear conscience toward God and men.

Acts 24:16 Holman CSB

Your conscience is a little feeling that will usually tell you what to do and when to do it. Pay attention to that feeling, and trust it.

If you slow down and listen to your conscience, you'll usually stay out of trouble. And if you listen to your conscience, it won't be so hard to control your own behavior. Why? Because most of the time, your conscience already knows right from wrong. So don't be in such a hurry to do things. Instead of "jumping right in," listen to your conscience. In the end, you'll be very glad you did.

Sleep On It!

If you're not sure what to do . . . slow down and listen to your conscience. That little voice inside your head is very dependable, but you can't depend upon it if you never listen to it. So stop, listen, and learn—your conscience is almost always right!

See the Good in Others

See to it that no one repays evil for evil to anyone, but always pursue what is good for one another and for all.

I Thessalonians 5:15 Holman CSB

Do you ever make mistakes? Of course you do! Even if you're a very good person, you're bound to make a mistake or two—everybody does.

When you do something you shouldn't have done, here are some things you can do:
1. Apologize to the people you've hurt, and ask for their forgiveness; 2. Fix the things you've messed up or broken; 3. Don't make the same mistake again; 4. Ask God for His forgiveness (which, by the way, He will give to you instantly); 5. Get busy doing something you can be proud of. 6. Don't be too hard on yourself . . . even if you made a mistake, you're still a very, very special person!

Sleep On It!

God forgives sin when you ask . . . so ask! God stands ready to forgive . . . the next move is yours.

Bedtime Devotional 309

A Pure Heart

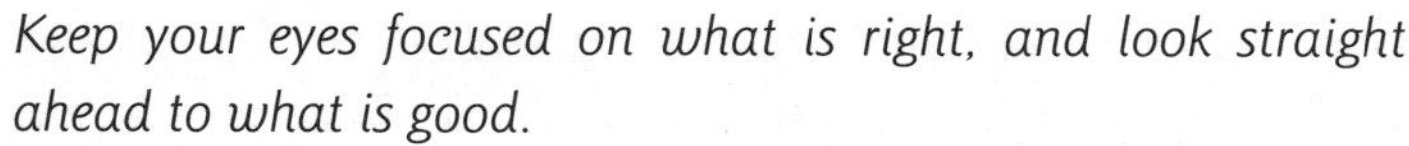

Keep your eyes focused on what is right, and look straight ahead to what is good.

Proverbs 4:25 NCV

Where does a good attitude begin? It starts in our hearts and works its way out from there. Jesus taught us that a pure heart is a wonderful blessing. It's up to each of us to fill our hearts with love for God, love for Jesus, and love for all people. When we do, good things happen.

Sometimes, of course, we don't feel much like feeling good. Sometimes, when we're tired, or frustrated, or angry, we simply don't want to have a good attitude. On those days when we're feeling bad, it's time to calm down . . . and rest up.

Do you want to be the best person you can be? Then you shouldn't grow tired of doing the right things . . . and you shouldn't ever grow tired of thinking the right thoughts.

Sleep On It!

Learn about Jesus and His attitude. Then try and do what Jesus would do.

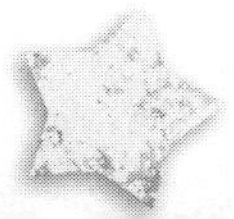

Blessed to Be a Blessing

God has given gifts to each of you from his great variety of spiritual gifts. Manage them well so that God's generosity can flow through you.

1 Peter 4:10 NLT

Jesus said, "It is more blessed to give than to receive." That means that we should be generous with other people—but sometimes we don't feel much like sharing. Instead of sharing the things that we have, we want to keep them all to ourselves. That's when we must remember that God doesn't want selfishness to rule our hearts; He wants us to be generous.

Are you lucky enough to have nice things? If so, God's instructions are clear: you must share your blessings with others. And that's exactly the way it should be. After all, think how generous God has been with you.

Sleep On It!

Too many toys? Give them away! Are you one of those lucky kids who has more toys than you can play with? If so, remember that not everyone is so lucky. Ask your parents to help you give some of your toys to children who need them more than you do.

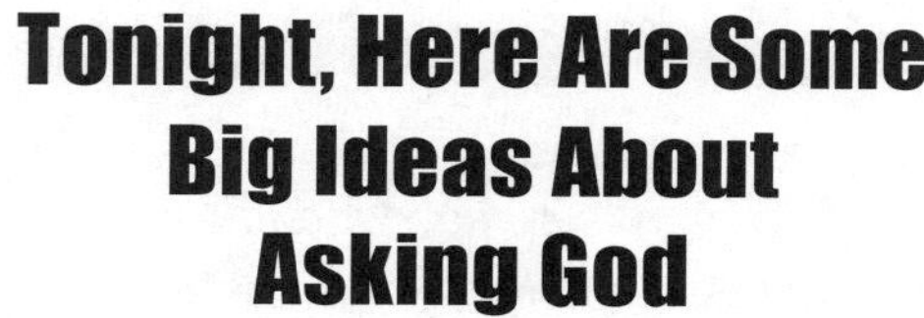

Tonight, Here Are Some Big Ideas About Asking God

Here are two important ideas. Take a few minutes to talk to your mom or dad about what these quotations mean.

If you want more from life, ask more from God.

Marie T. Freeman

Some people think God does not like to be troubled
with our constant asking.
But, the way to trouble God is not to come at all.

D. L. Moody

Bedtime Devotional 312

It's Not Hard to Be Kind

Therefore, God's chosen ones, holy and loved, put on heartfelt compassion, kindness, humility, gentleness, and patience.

Colossians 3:12 Holman CSB

How hard is it to say a kind word? Not very! Yet sometimes we're so busy that we forget to say the very things that might make other people feel better.

We should always try to say nice things to our families and friends. And when we feel like saying something that's not so nice, perhaps we should stop and think before we say it. Kind words help; cruel words hurt. It's as simple as that. And, when we say the right thing at the right time, we give a gift that can change someone's day or someone's life.

Sleep On It!

It's good to tell your family how you feel about them, but that's not enough. You should also show them how you feel with your good deeds and your kind words.

Obeying God and Happiness

I will praise you, Lord, with all my heart. I will tell all the miracles you have done. I will be happy because of you; God Most High, I will sing praises to your name.

Psalm 9:1-2 NCV

Do you want to be happy? Here are some things you should do: Love God and His Son, Jesus; obey the Golden Rule; and always try to do the right thing. When you do these things, you'll discover that happiness goes hand-in-hand with good behavior.

The happiest people do not misbehave; the happiest people are not cruel or greedy. The happiest people don't say unkind things. The happiest people are those who love God and follow His rules—starting, of course, with the Golden one.

Sleep On It!

Even if you're a very good person, you shouldn't expect to be happy all the time. Sometimes, things will happen to make you sad, and it's okay to be sad when bad things happen to you or to your friends and family. But remember: through good times and bad, you'll always be happier if you obey the rules of your Father in heaven. So obey them!

Bedtime Devotional 314

God Knows My Heart

Create in me a pure heart, God, and make my spirit right again.

Psalm 51:10 NCV

Other people see you from the outside. God sees you from the inside—God sees your heart.

Kindness comes from the heart. So does sharing. So if you want to show your family and your friends that your heart is filled with kindness and love, one way to do it is by sharing. But don't worry about trying to show God what kind of person you are. He already knows your heart, and He loves you more than you can imagine.

Sleep On It!

The God who dwells in heaven is willing to dwell also in the heart of the humble believer.

Warren Wiersbe

Honesty Begins At Home

Good people will be guided by honesty.

Proverbs 11:3 ICB

Should you be honest with your parents? Certainly. With your brothers and sisters? Of course. With cousins, grandparents, aunts, and uncles? Yes! In fact, you should be honest with everybody in your family because honesty starts at home.

If you can't be honest in your own house, how can you expect to be honest in other places, like at church or at school? So make sure that you're completely honest with your family. If you are, then you're much more likely to be honest with everybody else.

Sleep On It!

Sometimes, it's better to say nothing. If you're tempted to say something that isn't true, don't say anything. A closed mouth tells no lies.

Bedtime Devotional 316

The Joyful Life

Always be full of joy in the Lord. I say it again—rejoice!

Philippians 4:4 NLT

A man named C. S. Lewis once said, "Joy is the serious business of heaven." And he was right! God seriously wants you to be a seriously joyful person.

One way that you can have a more joyful life is by learning how to become a more obedient person. When you do, you'll stay out of trouble, and you'll have lots more time for fun.

So here's a way to be a more joyful, happy person: do the right thing! It's the best way to live.

Sleep On It!

Joy comes not from what we have but from what we are.

C. H. Spurgeon

Sharing Love and Kindness

Talk and act like a person expecting to be judged by the Rule that sets us free. For if you refuse to act kindly, you can hardly expect to be treated kindly. Kind mercy wins over harsh judgment every time.

James 2:12-13 MSG

Where does kindness start? It starts in our hearts and works its way out from there. Jesus taught us that a pure heart is a wonderful blessing. It's up to each of us to fill our hearts with love for God, love for Jesus, and love for all people. When we do, we are blessed.

Do you want to be the best person you can be? Then invite the love of Christ into your heart and share His love with your family and friends. And remember that lasting love always comes from a pure heart . . . like yours!

Sleep On It!

Everybody is important to God. And you should treat every person with courtesy, dignity and respect.

Bedtime Devotional 318

Tonight, Try to Memorize This Verse

For the wages of sin is death,
but the gift of God is eternal life
in Christ Jesus our Lord.

Romans 6:23 NIV

This is an important Bible verse. Practice saying it several times. And then, talk to your mom or dad about exactly what the verse means . . .

A Tip for Parents

Tonight, talk to your child about . . .
God's promise of eternal life.

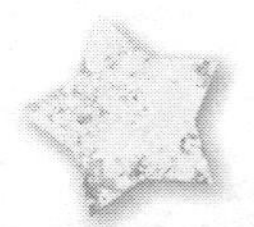

Bedtime Devotional 319

Living by God's Rules

Does the LORD delight in burnt offerings and sacrifices as much as in obeying the voice of the LORD? To obey is better than sacrifice . . . .

I Samuel 15:22 NIV

God has rules, and He wants you to obey them. He wants you to be fair, honest, and kind. He wants you to behave yourself, and He wants you to respect your parents. God has other rules, too, and you'll find them in a very special book: the Bible.

With a little help from your parents, you can figure out God's rules. And then, it's up to you to live by them. When you do, everybody will be pleased—you'll be pleased, your parents will be pleased . . . and God will be pleased, too.

Sleep On It!

When you obey God, you will feel better about yourself. When you don't obey Him, you will feel worse.

Bedtime Devotional 320

When Bad Things Happen

I leave you peace; my peace I give you. I do not give it to you as the world does. So don't let your hearts be troubled or afraid.

John 14:27 NCV

When bad things happen, it's understandable that we might feel afraid. In fact, it's good to be afraid if our fears keep us from behaving foolishly (by the way, if that little voice inside your head tells you that doing something is dangerous, don't do it).

When our own troubles—or the world's troubles—leave us fearful, we should discuss our concerns with the people who love and care for us. Parents and grandparents can help us understand our fears, and they can help us feel better. That's why we need to talk with them.

It's okay to be afraid—all of us are fearful from time to time. And it's good to know that we can talk about our fears with loved ones and with God. When we do, we'll discover that fear lasts for a little while, but love lasts forever.

Sleep On It!

Trust God to handle those problems that are simply too big for you to solve. And always talk to your parents about your fears.

Bedtime Devotional 321

Follow Jesus

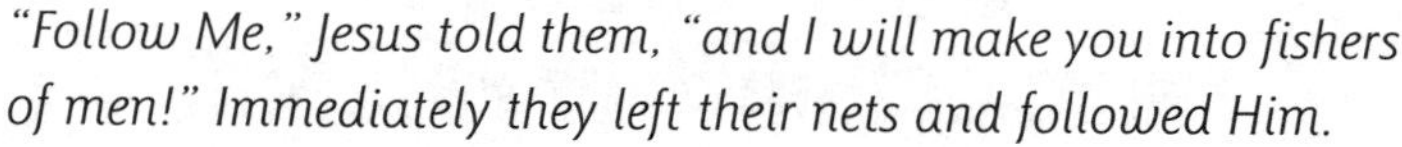

"Follow Me," Jesus told them, "and I will make you into fishers of men!" Immediately they left their nets and followed Him.

Mark 1:17-18 Holman CSB

Tomorrow morning when you wake up, who will you walk with? Do yourself a favor—walk with Jesus! God's Word promises that when you follow in Christ's footsteps, you will learn how to behave yourself, and you'll learn how to live a good life. Jesus wants you to be a "new creation" through Him. And that's exactly what you should want for yourself, too. So talk with Jesus (through prayer) and walk with Him (by obeying His rules) today and forever.

Sleep On It!

If you want to be a disciple of Christ . . . follow in His footsteps, obey His commandments, talk with Him often, tell others about Him, and share His never-ending love.

Bedtime Devotional 322

Tonight, Here Are Some Big Ideas About Respecting Your Parents

Here are two important ideas. Take a few minutes to talk to your mom or dad about what these quotations mean.

> How wonderful it is when parents and children respect each other . . . and show it.
>
> Jim Gallery

> The child who does not learn to obey his parents is not likely to grow up obeying any authority.
>
> Warren Wiersbe

Listen to God

Continue to ask, and God will give to you. Continue to search, and you will find. Continue to knock, and the door will open for you.

Matthew 7:7 ICB

God has many things He wants to tell us. And for starters, He wants us to be loving, kind, and patient, not rude or mean!

The Bible tells us that God is love and that if we wish to know Him, we must have love in our hearts. Sometimes, of course, when we're tired, angry, or frustrated, it is very hard for us to be loving. Thankfully, anger and frustration are feelings that come and go, but God's love lasts forever.

If you'd like to become a more patient person, talk to God in prayer, listen to what He says, and share His love with your family and friends. God is always listening, and He's ready to talk to you . . . now!

Sleep On It!

If you want more from life, ask more from God: D. L. Moody observed, "Some people think God does not like to be troubled with our constant asking. But, the way to trouble God is not to come at all."

Tonight, Try to Memorize This Verse

A cheerful heart
has a continual feast.

Proverbs 15:15 Holman CSB

This is an important Bible verse. Practice saying it several times. And then, talk to your mom or dad about exactly what the verse means . . .

A Tip for Parents

Tonight, talk to your child about . . .
the benefits of a happy heart.

Bedtime Devotional 325

Golden Rule

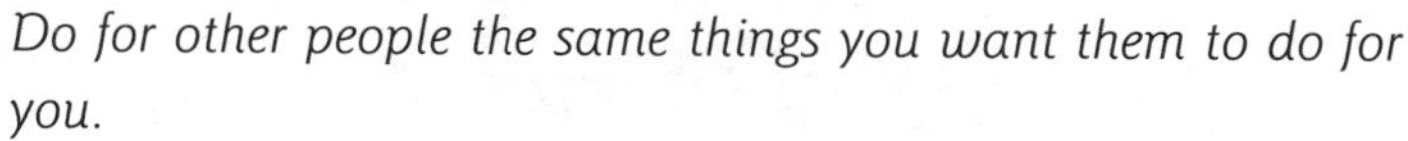

Do for other people the same things you want them to do for you.

Matthew 7:12 ICB

Some rules are easier to understand than they are to live by. Jesus told us that we should treat other people in the same way that we would want to be treated: that's the Golden Rule. But sometimes, especially when we're tired or upset, that rule is very hard to follow.

Jesus wants us to treat other people with respect, kindness, courtesy, and love. When we do, we make our families and friends happy . . . and we make our Father in heaven very proud.

Sleep On It!

The #1 rule of friendship is the Golden one.

Jim Gallery

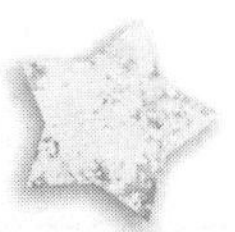

Tonight, Here Are Some Big Ideas About Putting Things Off Until the Last Minute

Here are two important ideas. Take a few minutes to talk to your mom or dad about what these quotations mean.

Every time you refuse to face up to life
and its problems, you weaken your character.

E. Stanley Jones

Do the unpleasant work first and enjoy the rest of the day.

Marie T. Freeman

Think Good Thoughts

Come near to God, and God will come near to you. You sinners, clean sin out of your lives. You who are trying to follow God and the world at the same time, make your thinking pure.

James 4:8 NCV

Do you try to think good thoughts about your friends, your family, and yourself? The Bible says that you should. Do you lift your hopes and your prayers to God many times each day? The Bible says that you should. Do you say "no" to people who want you to do bad things or think bad thoughts? The Bible says that you should.

The Bible teaches you to guard your thoughts against things that are hurtful or wrong. So remember this: When you turn away from bad thoughts and turn instead toward God and His Son Jesus, you will be protected . . . and you will be blessed.

Sleep On It!

Good thoughts can lead you to some very good places . . . and bad thoughts can lead elsewhere.

Bedtime Devotional 328

Tonight, Try to Memorize This Verse

Cast all your anxiety on him
because he cares for you.

I Peter 5:7 NIV

This is an important Bible verse. Practice saying it several times. And then, talk to your mom or dad about exactly what the verse means . . .

A Tip for Parents

Tonight, talk to your child about . . .
trusting God.

Bedtime Devotional 329

Telling the Truth

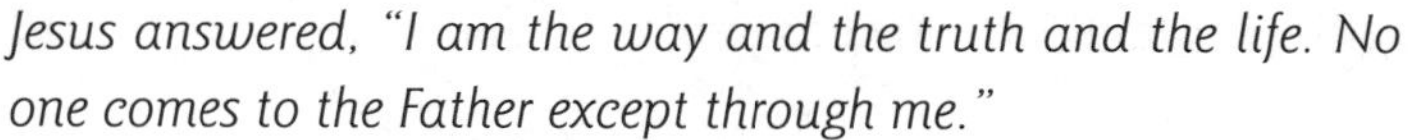

Jesus answered, "I am the way and the truth and the life. No one comes to the Father except through me."

John 14:6 NIV

Sometimes, telling the truth is hard, but even then, it's easier to tell the truth than it is to live with the consequences of telling a lie. You see, telling a lie can be easier in the beginning, but it's always harder in the end! In the end, when people find out that you've been untruthful, they may feel hurt and you will feel embarrassed.

So make this promise to yourself, and keep it: don't let lies rob you of your happiness. Instead, tell the truth from the start. You'll be doing yourself a big favor, and you'll be obeying the Word of God.

Sleep On It!

Those who walk in truth walk in liberty.

Beth Moore

Bedtime Devotional 330

The Best Day

This is the day the LORD has made. We will rejoice and be glad in it.

Psalm 118:24 NLT

What is the best day to celebrate life? This one! This day and every day should be a time for celebration as we think about all the things God has done for us.

Tomorrow morning, when you wake up, take time to count your blessings. And then, be sure to enjoy yourself. Each and every day is a gift from your Heavenly Father . . . SO CELEBRATE!

Sleep On It!

While you're celebrating life, don't try and keep the celebration to yourself. Let other people know why you're rejoicing, and don't be bashful about telling them how they can rejoice, too.

Bedtime Devotional 331

Tonight, Here Are Some Big Ideas About Celebrating Today

Here are two important ideas. Take a few minutes to talk to your mom or dad about what these quotations mean.

> Don't waste today's time cluttering up tomorrow's opportunities with yesterday's troubles.
>
> Barbara Johnson

> With each new dawn, life delivers a package to your front door, rings your doorbell, and runs.
>
> Charles Swindoll

Love Everybody

But love ye your enemies, and do good, and lend, hoping for nothing again; and your reward shall be great, and ye shall be the children of the Highest . . . .

Luke 6:35 KJV

It's easy to love people who have been nice to you, but it's very hard to love people who have treated you badly. Still, Jesus instructs us to treat both our friends and our enemies with kindness and respect.

Are you having problems being nice to someone? Is there someone you know whom you don't like very much? Remember that Jesus not only forgave His enemies, He also loved them . . . and so should you.

Sleep On It!

How hard is it to love your enemies? You'll never know until you try . . . so try!

An Example for Others

We're Christ's representatives. God uses us to persuade men and women to drop their differences and enter into God's work of making things right between them. We're speaking for Christ himself now: Become friends with God; he's already a friend with you.

2 Corinthians 5:20 MSG

What kind of example are you? Are you the kind of boy who shows other people what it means to be kind and forgiving? Hopefully so!!!

How hard is it to say a kind word? Not very! How hard is it to accept someone's apology? Usually not too hard. So today, be a good example for others to follow. Because God needs people, like you, who are willing to stand up and be counted for Him. And that's exactly the kind of example you should try to be.

Sleep On It!

Your behavior speaks volumes about your relationship with God.

Tonight, Try to Memorize This Verse

It is good and pleasant when
God's people live together in peace!

Psalm 133:1 NCV

This is an important Bible verse. Practice saying it several times. And then, talk to your mom or dad about exactly what the verse means . . .

A Tip for Parents

Tonight, talk to your child about . . .
. . . how to live with family and friends.

Bedtime Devotional 335

The Roadblock

Those who show mercy to others are happy, because God will show mercy to them.

Matthew 5:7 NCV

If you're unwilling to forgive other people, you're building a roadblock between yourself and God. And the less you're willing to forgive, the bigger your roadblock.

If you really want to forgive someone, pray for that person. And then pray for yourself by asking God to help you forgive. Don't expect forgiveness to be easy or quick, but with God as your helper, you can forgive . . . and you will.

Sleep On It!

God calls upon the loved not just to love but to be loving. God calls upon the forgiven not just to forgive but to be forgiving.

Beth Moore

Bedtime Devotional 336

The Wonder of Heaven

Be glad and rejoice, because your reward is great in heaven.

Matthew 5:12 Holman CSB

The Bible makes this important promise: when you give your heart to Jesus, you will live forever with Him in heaven. And Jesus told us that His house has "many mansions" (John 14:1-3).

Even though we don't know everything about heaven, we do know this: heaven will be a wonderful place, a place of joy and wonder, a place where we will be reunited with our loved ones and with God. It's wonderful to think about . . . and a priceless gift from God.

Sleep On It!

The main joy of heaven will be the Heavenly Father greeting us in a time and place of rejoicing, celebration, joy, and great reunion.

Bill Bright

Bedtime Devotional 337

Telling the Truth

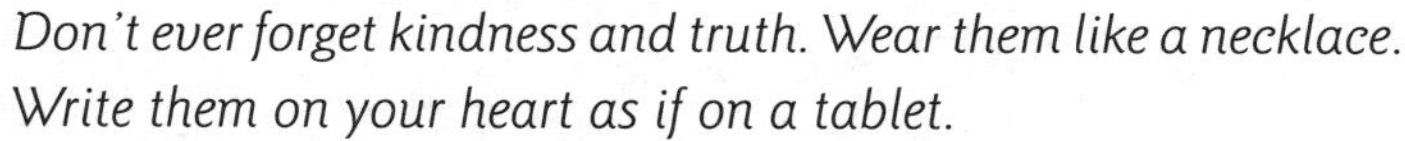

Don't ever forget kindness and truth. Wear them like a necklace. Write them on your heart as if on a tablet.

Proverbs 3:3 NCV

When we're dishonest, we make ourselves unhappy and we let other people down. It's easy to see that lies always cause far more problems than they solve. Lies, no matter what size, are never part of God's plan for our lives, so we must tell the truth about everything.

Have you ever said something that wasn't true? When you did, were you sorry for what you had said? Probably so.

Happiness and honesty always go hand in hand. But it's up to you to make sure that you go hand in hand with them! And besides, when you always tell the truth, you don't have to try and remember what it was that you said!

Sleep On It!

A lie is like a snowball: the further you roll it, the bigger it becomes.

Martin Luther

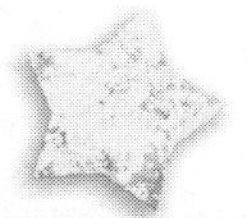

Bedtime Devotional 338

Kindness Is a Choice

Love is patient; love is kind.

I Corinthians 13:4 Holman CSB

Kindness is a choice. Sometimes, when we feel happy or hopeful, we find it easy to be kind. Other times, when we are sad or tired, we may find it much harder to be kind. But the Bible teaches us to be kind, even when we don't feel like it.

So do everybody (including yourself) a big favor: try to be kind all the time. It's the smart choice and the right thing to do.

Sleep On It!

Kindness should be part of our lives every day, not just on the days when we feel good. And remember: small acts of kindness can make a big difference.

Bedtime Devotional 339

Do the Right Thing . . . And the Kind Thing

Let everyone see that you are gentle and kind. The Lord is coming soon.

Philippians 4:5 NCV

Sometimes, it's so much easier to do the wrong thing than it is to do the right thing, especially when we're tired or frustrated. But, doing the wrong thing almost always leads to trouble. And sometimes, it leads to BIG trouble.

When you do the right thing, you don't have to worry about what you did or what you said. But, when you do the wrong thing, you'll be worried that someone will find out. So do the right thing, which, by the way, also happens to be the kind thing. You'll be glad you did, and so will other people!

Sleep On It!

When you launch an act of kindness out into the crosswinds of life, it will blow kindness back to you.

Dennis Swanberg

Bedtime Devotional 340

Tonight, Here Are Some Big Ideas About Helping Others

Here are two important ideas. Take a few minutes to talk to your mom or dad about what these quotations mean.

Encouraging others means helping people,
looking for the best in them,
and trying to bring out their positive qualities.
John Maxwell

Make it a rule, and pray to God to help you to keep it, never, if possible, to lie down at night without being able to say: "I have made one human being at least a little wiser, or a little happier, or at least a little better this day."
Charles Kingsley

Bedtime Devotional 341

Learning the Importance of Obedience

You must follow the Lord your God and fear Him. You must keep His commands and listen to His voice; you must worship Him and remain faithful to Him.

Deuteronomy 13:4 Holman CSB

When you learn to control your actions and your words, you will find it easier to obey your parents, your teachers, and your Father in heaven. Why? Because in order to be an obedient person, you must first learn how to control yourself—otherwise, you won't be able to obey very well, even when you want to.

When you learn the importance of obedience, you'll soon discover that good things happen when you behave yourself. And the sooner you learn to listen and obey, the sooner those good things will start happening.

Sleep On It!

What about all the rules you learn about in the Bible? Well, those aren't just any old rules—they're God's rules. And you should behave—and obey—accordingly.

Want More Patience? God Can Help!

Smart people are patient; they will be honored if they ignore insults.

Proverbs 19:11 NCV

Are you a perfectly patient person? If so, feel free to skip the rest of this page. But if you're not, here's something to think about: If you really want to become a more patient person, God is ready and willing to help.

God is always ready to help you become a better person. In fact, the Bible promises that when you sincerely seek God's help, He will give you the things you need. So, if you want to become a more patient person, bow your head and start praying about it. Then, rest assured that with God's help, you can change for the better . . . and you will!

Sleep On It!

Patience pays. Impatience costs.

Criswell Freeman

Bedtime Devotional 343

Christ's Peace

Peace I leave with you. My peace I give to you. I do not give to you as the world gives. Your heart must not be troubled or fearful.

John 14:27 Holman CSB

The beautiful words of John 14:27 remind us that Jesus offers us peace, not as the world gives, but as He alone gives. We, as believers, can accept His peace or ignore it. When we accept the peace of Jesus Christ into our hearts, our lives are changed forever, and we become more loving, patient Christians.

Christ's peace is offered freely; it has been already paid for; it is ours for the asking. So let us ask . . . and then share.

Sleep On It!

Genuine peace is a gift from God. Your job is to accept it.

Tonight, Here Are Some Big Ideas About Being Joyful

Here are two important ideas. Take a few minutes to talk to your mom or dad about what these quotations mean.

Christ and joy go together.

E. Stanley Jones

Our sense of joy, satisfaction, and fulfillment in life
increases, no matter what the circumstances,
if we are in the center of God's will.

Billy Graham

Bedtime Devotional 345

The Time to Talk to God Is Now

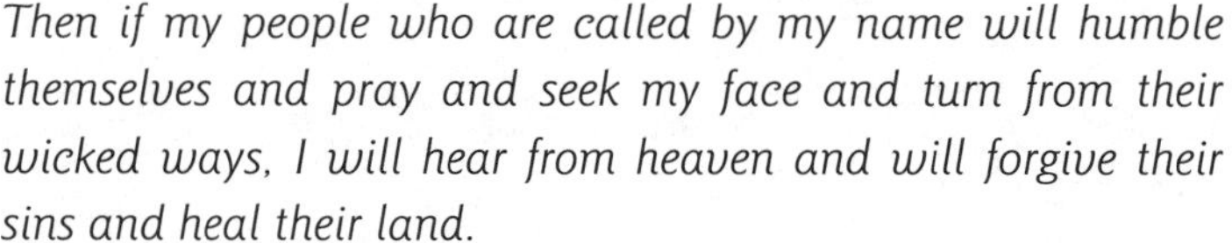

Then if my people who are called by my name will humble themselves and pray and seek my face and turn from their wicked ways, I will hear from heaven and will forgive their sins and heal their land.

2 Chronicles 7:14 NLT

God promises that He hears your prayers—every one of them! So if you want to say something to God, you can start praying (with your eyes open or shut).

Whatever your need, no matter how great or small, pray about it and never lose hope. God is not just near; He is here, and He's ready to talk with you. Now!

Sleep On It!

Sometimes, the answer to prayer is "No." God doesn't grant all of our requests, nor should He.

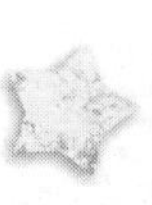

Don't Be Afraid to Ask Questions

When doubts filled my mind, your comfort gave me renewed hope and cheer.

Psalm 94:19 NLT

When you're not sure about something, are you willing to ask your parents what you should do? Hopefully, when you have a question, you're not afraid to ask.

If you've got lots of questions, the Bible promises that God—like your parents—has answers, too.

So don't ever be afraid to ask questions. Both your parents and your Heavenly Father want to hear your questions . . . and they want to answer your questions as soon as you ask.

Sleep On It!

When in doubt, ask Mom or Dad: If you're not sure whether something is right or wrong, ask your parents before you do it!

Self-Control Matters

So prepare your minds for service and have self-control. All your hope should be for the gift of grace that will be yours when Jesus Christ is shown to you.

1 Peter 1:13 NCV

Learning how to control yourself is an important part of growing up. The more you learn about self-control, the better. Self-control will help you at home, at school, and at church. That's why parents and teachers are happy to talk about the rewards of good self-control. And that's why you should be excited about learning how important it is to look before you leap . . . not after!

Sleep On It!

Sometimes, the best way to control yourself is to slow yourself down. Then, you can think about the things you're about to do before you do them.

Yes, Jesus Loves You!

You're blessed when you're content with just who you are—no more, no less. That's the moment you find yourselves proud owners of everything that can't be bought.

Matthew 5:5 MSG

Have you heard the song "Jesus Loves Me"? Probably so. It's a happy song that should remind you of this important fact: Jesus loves you very much.

When you invite Jesus into your heart, He'll protect you forever. If you have problems, He'll help you solve them. When you aren't perfect, He'll still love you. If you feel sorry or sad, He can help you feel better.

Yes, Jesus loves you . . . and you should love yourself. So the next time you feel sad about yourself . . . or something that you've done . . . remember that Jesus loves you, your family loves you, and you should feel that way, too.

Sleep On It!

Nobody else in the world is exactly like you. When God made you, He made a very special, one-of-a-kind person. So don't forget this fact: you're very, very, very, very, very special.

Friends Should Share

The righteous give without sparing.

Proverbs 21:26 NIV

How can you be a good friend? One way is by sharing. And here are some of the things you can share: smiles, kind words, pats on the back, your toys, school supplies, books, and, of course, your prayers.

Would you like to make your friends happy? And would you like to make yourself happy at the same time? Here's how: treat your friends like you want to be treated. That means obeying the Golden Rule, which, of course, means sharing. In fact, the more you share, the better friend you'll be.

Sleep On It!

Sharing with guests is an important way to demonstrate hospitality.

Martha and Mary

But Martha was pulled away by all she had to do in the kitchen. Later, she stepped in, interrupting them. "Master, don't you care that my sister has abandoned the kitchen to me? Tell her to lend me a hand." The Master said, "Martha, dear Martha, you're fussing far too much and getting yourself worked up over nothing. One thing only is essential, and Mary has chosen it—it's the main course, and won't be taken from her."

Luke 10:40-42 MSG

Okay, after that rather long Bible passage, your devotional is almost up, so we'll make it short and sweet: Martha was concerned with doing things for Jesus. Mary was concerned with being with Jesus. Mary made the better choice. Why? Because we need to be with Christ before we start doing things for Him. End of lesson.

Sleep On It!

When we are in a situation where Jesus is all we have, we soon discover He is all we really need.

Gigi Graham Tchividjian

Tonight, Try to Memorize This Verse

Jesus answered, I am the way and the truth and the life. No-one comes to the Father except through me.

John 4:16 NIV

This is an important Bible verse. Practice saying it several times. And then, talk to your mom or dad about exactly what the verse means . . .

A Tip for Parents

Tonight, talk to your child about . . .
God's promise of eternal life.

Bedtime Devotional 352

Think About the Other Person

I pray that your love for each other will overflow more and more, and that you will keep on growing in your knowledge and understanding.

Philippians 1:9 NLT

There's an old saying that goes something like this: "Try to put yourself in the other person's shoes." It means that the more you understand somebody, the easier it is to forgive that person.

When you become angry with someone, try putting yourself in the other person's shoes. When you do, perhaps you'll be a little bit more understanding—and a little bit quicker to forgive.

Sleep On It!

Kindness starts at home. So, it's important for you to be understanding of all your family members.

The Right Time

He has made everything beautiful in its time. He has also set eternity in the hearts of men; yet they cannot fathom what God has done from beginning to end.

Ecclesiastes 3:11 NIV

Sometimes, the hardest thing to do is to wait. This is especially true when we're in a hurry and when we want things to happen now, if not sooner! But God's plan does not always happen in the way that we would like or at the time of our own choosing. Still, God always knows best.

Sometimes, even though we may want something very badly, we must still be patient and wait for the right time to get it. And the right time, of course, is determined by God, not by us.

Sleep On It!

Even when you want events to unfold according to your own timetable, it is important to trust God's timetable.

Tonight, Here Are Some Big Ideas About The Words You Speak

Here are two important ideas. Take a few minutes to talk to your mom or dad about what these quotations mean.

I still believe we ought to talk about Jesus.
The old country doctor of my boyhood days always began
his examination by saying, "Let me see your tongue."
That's a good way to check a Christian: the tongue test.
Let's hear what he is talking about.

Vance Havner

Change the heart, and you change the speech.

Warren Wiersbe

When Things Go Wrong

I do not consider myself yet to have taken hold of it. But one thing I do: Forgetting what is behind and straining toward what is ahead, I press on toward the goal to win the prize for which God has called me heavenward in Christ Jesus.

Philippians 3:13-14 NIV

When things don't turn out right, it's easy for most of us to give up. Why are we tempted to give up so quickly? Perhaps it's because we're afraid that we might embarrass ourselves if we tried hard but didn't succeed.

If you're having a little trouble getting something done, don't get mad, don't get frustrated, don't get discouraged, and don't give up. Just keep trying and believing in yourself.

When you try hard you can do amazing things . . . but if you quit at the first sign of trouble, you'll miss out. So here's a good rule to follow: when you have something that you want to finish, be brave enough (and wise enough) to finish it . . . you'll feel better about yourself when you do.

Sleep On It!

Even if you can't see a perfect solution today, you may stumble over a perfect solution tomorrow, so don't give up at the first sign of trouble.

Bedtime Devotional 356

Are You Feeling Upset or Worried? Pray About It!

I want men everywhere to lift up holy hands in prayer, without anger or disputing.

I Timothy 2:8 NIV

If you're feeling upset, what should you do? Well, you should talk to your parents and there's something else you can do: you can pray about it.

If there is person you don't like, you should pray for a forgiving heart. If there is something you're worried about, you should ask God to give you comfort. And as you pray more, you'll discover that God is always near and that He's always ready to hear from you. So don't worry about things; pray about them. God is waiting patiently to hear from you . . . and He's ready to listen NOW!

Sleep On It!

One way to make sure that your heart is in tune with God is to pray often. The more you talk to God, the more He will talk to you.

When We Don't Understand

Immediately the father of the child cried out and said with tears, "Lord, I believe; help my unbelief!"

Mark 9:24 NKJV

Even a good man like Moses couldn't always understand the mysteries of God's plans. And neither can we. Sometimes, people who do nothing wrong get sick; sometimes, innocent people are hurt; sometimes, bad things happen to very good people. And just like Moses, we can't always understand why.

But the good news is this: We will have an eternity to have all our questions answered when we get to heaven. And until then, we've simply got to trust God.

Sleep On It!

If you're afraid to raise your hand and ask a question, remember this . . . if you don't understand something, lots of other people in the classroom probably don't understand it, either. So you'll be doing everybody a big favor if you raise your hand and ask your question.

Learning to Be More Obedient

Here is my final advice: Honor God and obey his commands.

Ecclesiastes 12:13 ICB

Learning how to control yourself helps you become a more obedient person. So the more you learn about self-control, the better.

Learning how to control yourself is a good thing. Self-control helps you at home, at school, and at church. That's why parents and teachers are happy to talk about the rewards of good behavior.

If you want to learn more about self-control, ask your parents. They'll help you figure out better ways to behave yourself. And that's good for everybody . . . especially you!

Sleep On It!

Be patient, and follow the rules. Even if you don't like some of the rules that you're supposed to follow, follow them anyway.

What Is Patience?

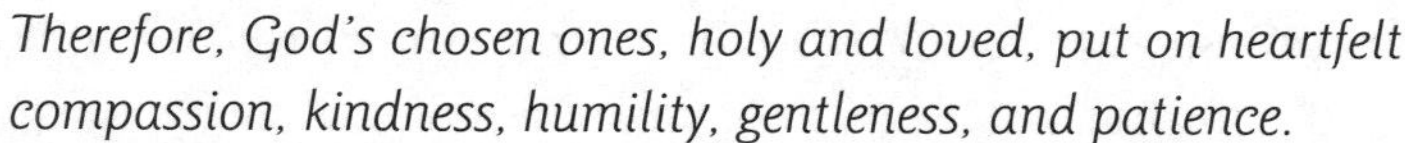

Therefore, God's chosen ones, holy and loved, put on heartfelt compassion, kindness, humility, gentleness, and patience.

Colossians 3:12 Holman CSB

The dictionary defines the word "patience" as "the ability to be calm, tolerant, and understanding." Here's what that means: the word "calm" means being in control of your emotions (not letting your emotions control you). The word "tolerant" means being kind and considerate to people who are different from you. And, the word "understanding" means being able to put yourself in another person's shoes.

If you can be calm, tolerant, and understanding, you will be the kind of person whose good deeds are a blessing to your family and friends. And that's exactly the kind of person that God wants you to be.

Sleep On It!

The best things in life seldom happen overnight . . . they usually take time.

The Right Thing

For the Kingdom of God is not just fancy talk; it is living by God's power.

I Corinthians 4:20 NLT

Doing the right thing is not always easy, especially when we're tired or frustrated. But, doing the wrong thing almost always leads to trouble. And sometimes, it leads to BIG trouble.

When you do the right thing, you don't have to worry about what you did or what you said. But, if you are dishonest—or if you do something that you know is wrong—you'll be worried that someone will find out. So do the right thing; it may be harder in the beginning, but it's easier in the end.

Sleep On It!

Nobody is good by accident.

C. H. Spurgeon

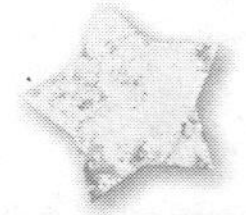

Bedtime Devotional 361

Tonight, Here Are Some Big Ideas About God's Plans

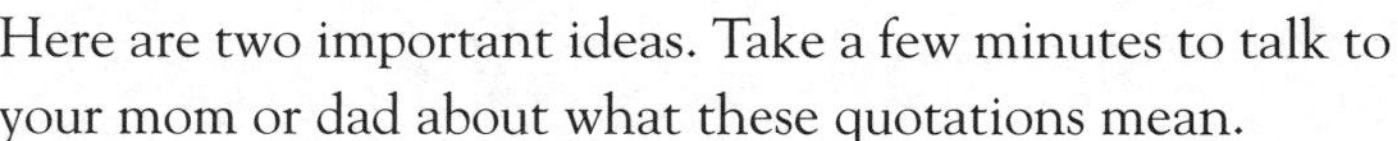

Here are two important ideas. Take a few minutes to talk to your mom or dad about what these quotations mean.

God will never lead you where
His strength cannot keep you.

Barbara Johnson

God is at work; He is in full control;
He is in the midst of whatever has happened,
is happening, and will happen.

Charles Swindoll

Bedtime Devotional 362

When Homework Should Be Done

We can't afford to waste a minute, must not squander these precious daylight hours in frivolity and indulgence, in sleeping around and dissipation, in bickering and grabbing everything in sight. Get out of bed and get dressed! Don't loiter and linger, waiting until the very last minute. Dress yourselves in Christ, and be up and about!

Romans 13:13-14 MSG

Sooner or later, you'll start getting homework, and when that day comes, you'd better be ready because that's when you'll really need lots of self-control! Usually, homework isn't hard to do, but it takes time. And sometimes, we'd rather be doing other things (like playing outside or watching TV). But, when we put off our homework until the last possible minute, we make it hard on ourselves.

Instead of putting off your homework, do it first. Then, you'll have the rest of your time to have fun—and you won't have to worry about all that homework.

Sleep On It!

Even a small step in the right direction is still a step in the right direction.

Giving to Your church

In everything I did, I showed you that by this kind of hard work we must help the weak, remembering the words the Lord Jesus himself said: "It is more blessed to give than to receive."

Acts 20:35 NIV

When the offering plate passes by, are you old enough to drop anything in it? If you are, congratulations! But if you're not quite old enough to give money to the church, don't worry—there are still lots of things you can share!

Even when you don't have money to share, you still have much to give to your church. What are some things you can share? Well, you can share your smile, your happiness, your laughter, your energy, your cooperation, your prayers, your obedience, your example, and your love.

So don't worry about giving to the church: even if you don't have lots of money, there are still plenty of ways you can give. And the best time to start giving is NOW!

Sleep On It!

What does the Bible say about sharing our possessions? The Bible answers this question very clearly: when other people need our help, we should gladly share the things we have.

Safety Matters

The prudent see danger and take refuge, but the simple keep going and suffer from it.

Proverbs 27:12 NIV

Self-control and safety go hand in hand. Why? Because a big part of self-control is looking around and thinking things through before you do something that you might regret later.

Remember the saying "Look before you leap!"? Well if you want to live safely and happily, you should look very carefully before you decide whether or not to leap. After all, it's easy to leap, but once you're in the middle of your jump, it's too late to leap back!

Sleep On It!

Don't complain about safety: whether it's a fire drill at school or wearing seat belts in the family car, don't whine, complain, or resist. When grown-ups are trying to keep you safe, your job is to help them do it!

What a Friend

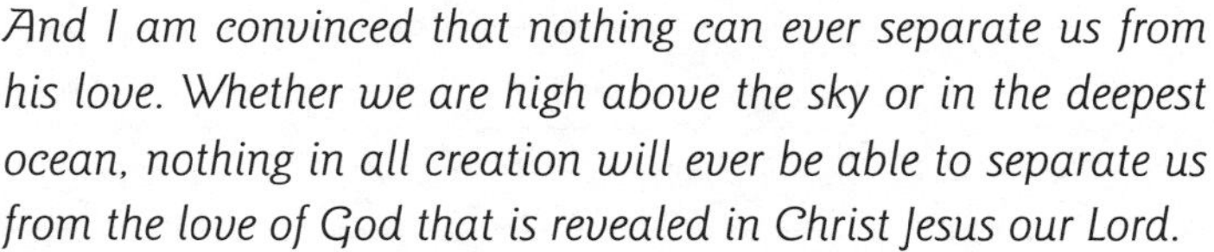

And I am convinced that nothing can ever separate us from his love. Whether we are high above the sky or in the deepest ocean, nothing in all creation will ever be able to separate us from the love of God that is revealed in Christ Jesus our Lord.

Romans 8:38–39 NLT

Jesus loves you very much. And you should love Him, too. When you invite Jesus into your heart, you can be sure that He will prepare a place for you in heaven.

Jesus has promised that heaven will be a wonderful place, a place where you will be protected forever.

Jesus is the best friend this world has ever known. Let Him be your friend, too. His love lasts forever. So, what are you waiting for? Welcome Him into your heart right now.

Sleep On It!

Jesus loves you. His love is amazing, it's wonderful, and it's meant for you.

My Notes and Things to Pray About

My Notes and Things to Pray About

My Notes and Things to Pray About

My Notes and Things to Pray About

My Notes and Things to Pray About

My Notes and Things to Pray About

My Notes and Things to Pray About

My Notes and Things to Pray About

My Notes and Things to Pray About